MW00526197

What People ~~are saying about~~
Coach Bob, *Unscatter the Chatter*, and the iMatter Process

Bob will show you why you matter and how self-discovery will unleash your best path forward.

—Ali Nasser
Author of *The Business Owner's Dilemma*

Bob's commitment to lifelong growth is culminated in this fast-reading book. He shares well-earned tools proven by himself and with other Visionaries for navigating the entrepreneurial journey. This is the Visionary guide to wisdom.

—John D. Anderson
Business Strategist, Entrepreneur, and
Founder EO Detroit Chapter
Author of *Replace Retirement:
Living Your Legacy in the Exponential Age*

This is a must-read! Coach Bob has done a wonderful job of putting together simple tools that can be applied to your life to make an immediate impact. My favorite tool, the daily 3-3-1™, helps you focus on the impact you can make by bringing clarity, intentionality, and reflection on what matters most in life. Keeping these things top of mind allows you to fully embrace your day. I am grateful Coach Bob helps us connect to ourselves!

—Kristie Clayton
Founder Female Integrator Mastermind (FIM),
Integrator iMatter & The Visionary Forum

Unscatter the Chatter is filled with valuable resources and insights to help us truly sort through the noise of our minds and gain greater clarity on what matters most. Bob's inspiring story of self-discovery and perseverance as well as his determination to never settle for less than he deserves serves as a beacon of possibility for us all. Don't just pick up the book and read it. Download the tools and take action to get clarity, shed the insignificant, and get in the driver's seat of your life.

—Mari Tautimes
Author of *#KeepGoing: From 15-Year-Old Mom to Successful CEO & Entrepreneur*

We as humans do not enter this world with an owner's manual, and one doesn't show up on our doorstep as adults either. Only *you* can create and own your personal owner's manual; it's inside you. It lies dormant for most people, just waiting to be let loose. The iMatter system helps you systematically connect your heart to your head and unlock your true life's journey. Take this key and go find your life.

—John J. Glon
Founder and Visionary, Great Lakes Essential Power

The mountain has invited me to create and live a legacy that is authentic to me, and I've owned the fact that once I'm authentic to myself and realize my true gifts, I can serve the world. It wrapped a whole lifetime into a little package of clarity and awesomeness. Coach Bob has the unique ability to observe and see my words when I am slipping into something that doesn't serve me. He has taught me a new way of being non-judgmental and accepting peoples' thoughts and appreciating them. I look at Coach Bob as a conduit to being open and accepting and to possibility thinking.

—Jill Young
Professional EOS Implementer®,
Author of the *Advantage* series

Going to the mountain was a fantastic experience. The fresh air, views, fitness, and opportunity to disconnect allowed me to get perspective on everything that's going on in my world and get clear on my priorities—what's most important to me. Trying to do that in the busyness of day-to-day life just wouldn't work. Coach Bob, I appreciate your coaching on a minute-to-minute basis, your power of observation, and learning from your example.

—Alex Freytag
Professional EOS Implementer®,
Author of Profit Works

Bob's facilitation of our forum's retreat, along with the iMatter tools, dramatically helped our EO forum get to a new, deeper level that has been fantastic. The lessons learned also helped me immensely with balance in my life and enhancing the relationships that matter most.

—Darton Case
President of DartAppraisal.com,
Past Chairman of EO Global Organization

The iMatter process fosters trust, deepens empathy, and eliminates organizational dysfunction that can lead to sub-optimal results. Coach Bob facilitated a multiday offsite for our senior management team. The team emerged ready to tackle any challenge together, and we grew the company +30 percent annually until we sold NEXTEP in 2018.

—Tommy Woycik
Former President, NEXTEP Systems

Bob has truly opened my mind by teaching me how vitally important spirituality is to achieving fulfillment and happiness. Through the iMatter process, I have learned to understand the possibilities that exist around me. As a result, I am able to welcome each day with more clarity and energy and enthusiasm. The iMatter process has helped to elevate my awareness of the power of relationships between individuals and the universe.

—Ted Haddad
Co-Founder, Azimuth Capital Management, LLC

For me, iMatter was a big game-changer. Coach Bob helped me to identify my North Star, allowing me to bring my leadership and personal life to another level. I became clear about what matters most and was able to let go of things that didn't. I highly recommend *Unscatter the Chatter*. Take a chance on it—it'll be worth it!

—Rob Dube
Co-CEO and Co-Founder, imageOne, and
Visionary for The 10 Disciplines with Gino Wickman

I learned from Coach Bob that if I wanted to be a great husband, father, brother, son, employer, and member of my community, I really needed to focus on myself. I set out on a journey using what I've learned from his books and the iMatter exercises. I identified who it was I wanted to be and, slowly but surely, I have achieved a place in life where I truly benefit others because I matter most.

I highly recommend Coach Bob and iMatter, as it is quite easy to lose that self-esteem and break touch with ourselves while paying more attention to others.

—Ivan Katz
Owner and Visionary, Great Lakes
Landscape Design Inc.

UNSCATTER THE CHATTER™

ELEVATE YOUR MIND
EXPAND YOUR IMPACT

UNSCATTER THE CHATTER™

ELEVATE YOUR MIND
EXPAND YOUR IMPACT

COACH BOB SHENEFELT

iMATTER

Published by Ethos Collective™
PO Box 43, Powell, OH 43065
EthosCollective.vip

LCCN: 2022913224
Paperback ISBN: 978-1-63680-086-8
Hardback ISBN: 978-1-63680-087-5
e-book ISBN: 978-1-63680-088-2

Available in paperback, hardback, and e-book.

Acknowledgments

To my wife, Sheryl, who has always believed in me, oftentimes more than I do: Thank you for continuing to choose us and providing me with love and support. You are my mirror, and you continually remind me that I matter!

To my kids, for learning with me and teaching me a lot of these simple practices. Thank you for calling me out when I need it and for being my greatest teachers.

To the members of the Entrepreneurial Organization (EO) and the EO forum, who encouraged me to share my fears, frustrations, dreams, and successes: Thank you especially to my forum, John Anderson, Curt Rager, Brian Ferrilla, Michael Berger, Michael Cauley, and Dan Glisky, for being there for me and creating a trusted space to hear myself think.

To my book club, Gino Wickman and Curt Rager: Thank you for allowing me to share my lessons and thoughts. Thank you for teaching me and for going to the mountain with me for over twenty years. I appreciate you for the unbelievable laughter and relentless pushing, pulling, and prodding.

To my iMatter partners, Chris Shenefelt and J.P. Hogan: Chris, thank you for believing in me, even when my message and plan were not yet clear. J.P., thank you for mentoring and inspiring me on the tools and lessons. I appreciate you both.

To my clients: You have trusted me, given feedback, and taught me many lessons. Thank you.

Contents

Part 2: Shift Your Mindset

Part 3: Commitment

Part 4: Clarity

Part 5: Confidence

Part 6: Enlightenment

Foreword

For over twenty years, I have taken an annual retreat to Boulder, Colorado, with two dear friends.

One is Curt Rager, and the other is the author of this amazing book, *Unscatter the Chatter*. The first time I went to Boulder with Bob, I will admit he freaked me out a little. Our spiritual conversations and his overtly expressing gratitude for the animals and nature on our hikes felt a little woo-woo to me.

I am now a convert. Bob opened my eyes and helped put this hard-charging, intense, entrepreneur "doer" on a spiritual path to becoming a hard-charging, intense, entrepreneur "being." I credit him for teaching me gratitude, which has had a huge impact on my life, along with introducing me to many incredible people and experiences that have brought me closer to my soul.

I am blown away as to how well Bob has packaged everything he's shared with Curt and me over the last twenty years into this wonderful book. He has also done a great job putting it all into his retreat experience, available to you, which he calls Go to the Mountain.

This book is a simple, fun read that is enlightening. Bob helps people connect with who they truly are. If that is something you are in search of, you are reading the right book.

Enjoy the journey.

—Gino Wickman
Founder and Creator of EOS Worldwide, and
Author of *Traction* and *Entrepreneurial Leap*

Note to the Reader

Look around you. Every living thing has a way of being in the world, an operating system—you included. Your operating system affects how you view life and how you do life.

Your life exists by design or default, choice or chance. Leave it up to chance, and maybe things will turn out okay, but that's a huge roll of the dice. Do you really want to tie your future to chance?

Me either. That's why my beautiful wife, Sheryl, and I created iMatter™ and are living the iMatter Journey™.

Welcome.

My name is Coach Bob, and my passion in life—my North Star—is to elevate the entrepreneurial spirit through self-mastery and connection. In living out my *why*, I am honored to empower people to live *great* f'ing lives—the kind of lives few people dare to dream about.

During the past four decades, I've helped men and women from around the world build incredible lives and businesses. They are leaders and entrepreneurs, husbands and wives, partners, parents, and friends, and some are even kids. In other words, they are just like you, with perhaps one key distinction: They have an extreme commitment to, clarity about, and confidence in the kind of life they want to lead—*and they are making it a reality.*

How? By living with intention and purpose. They are committed to using the process continuously and diving in to clarify why they are here on this planet, what they want to do with their time and energy, and how to impact their future so that it is greater than their past.

How about you? Are you fully satisfied with your life? Or are you living a life confined to have-tos instead of get-tos or, better yet, *love*-tos?

My guess is that you picked up or downloaded this book because your current life isn't the experience you want. As a kid, maybe you dreamed your life would be filled with never-ending magic and joy. Maybe some of the pieces are in place, but something is missing. You worry that you won't leave the legacy you'd planned or make the impact you'd hoped. You know there has to be *more*—even if you don't have clarity yet about what that *more* is.

If that is true for you, and you are ready to take the first steps on a journey toward the life you want, then you are in the right place, and this is the right book for you. My friend, the time is *now* for us to not only create a great future for ourselves but to enjoy the process—the adventure and the experience of being present right here and right *now*. No matter what stage of life you're stepping into (and we are all stepping into new stages in varying degrees), *now* is the time to realize and act like *you matter.*

Maybe you have felt scattered, stunted, or stuck in the past few years—or the past few decades. So many of us are still shaking off the fear, anger, and effects of isolation of 2020 and 2021. I know that I've felt angry at the abuse of power I've seen in leaders across the country and around the world. If I'm honest with myself, I can look back on the past couple of years and see where I've abdicated my power by slipping into habits of fear, anger, or complacency. Even though I *know* I have the power to choose an amazing life, sometimes that chatter in my head can be distracting and negative. That is not who I want to be, and that's not how I want to live.

In the process of writing this book, I experienced the refreshing and reviving clarity of remembering that I matter. Applying the tools I've successfully used with my coaching clients for decades, I recommitted myself to the iMatter Journey—a way of living that taps into my unique wisdom to elevate my mindset and expand my impact. By living with my *why*, *what*, and *how* (things you will clarify for yourself in the coming chapters), I re-centered myself and renewed my confidence that I am living my legacy right *now*. Simple, intentional shifts in my mindset have allowed me to experience life in a rhythm and flow that empowers me to be my best for myself and everyone around me.

It feels amazing; I feel like myself again. I am experiencing the freedom, love, and joy of living my truth. I want that for you as well!

In this book, we'll look at some simple yet profound wisdom about what it means to unscatter the chatter going on in your mind and find the clarity that will allow you to design and live life knowing and acting like you matter! We'll use the metaphor of an operating system because just like the operating system that runs your computer or your smartphone, the iMatter Journey is about keeping your personal world running at its best. Unique to you, it is a powerful combination of commitment, personal insight, new confidence, and self-mastery. This life operating system is straightforward and effective, and it equips you to live with purpose so you can create not just a *good* life but a *great* life.

Each time you apply the iMatter mindset to your life and use the tools in the iMatter Journey, you'll reaffirm that *you matter*. That belief is the first step to leaving behind a life of have-tos and enjoying a life of love-tos.

What are you waiting for?

Introduction: My First Lecture

When my father died many years ago, I was angry.

Of course, I was sad. I loved my dad. The anger arose from feeling abandoned. It seemed as if he had left me to fend for myself—with no written instructions or documented legacy to follow or live up to. I wanted to know more about who he was and what motivated him. I wanted him to have passed down his wisdom to me like a master teaches a disciple. I regretted that he died before I had the opportunity to ask all the questions I wanted to and learn all I could from him about his life experiences.

I worried about what I would say when it came time for me to speak at his funeral.

Then I stepped back from the anger of losing my dad, which was rooted in grief, and I thought about his life and my favorite memories with him. Memories like how no matter where he was, he would pull over on the side of the road

1

to watch a beautiful sunset and how he made time for family came to mind. It dawned on me that I was being unfair. My dad wasn't a teacher or a coach by profession, so he didn't always use words to instruct me. Instead, he taught by sharing what he loved with me and living his life around what mattered most to him. It turns out I just hadn't been paying attention to the amazing wisdom he had been living by example all along the way.

On the day of the funeral, I stepped to the podium and delivered a eulogy I titled "Dad's Top Ten Lessons for Living." (See page 187.) It's one of my favorite talks to give, and I still include it in my presentations all these years later to demonstrate how changing my thinking and perspective on life made a huge impact on my attitude and actions.

I'm thankful for the beautiful things my father taught me through his example—that is his legacy. Not surprisingly, speaking at his funeral caused me to reflect on what I want people to say about *me*—about my impact on their lives and the way I lived my life. What would my legacy be?

It is easy to get distracted by activity, the demands of others, or societal definitions of success. When that happens, we miss out on the opportunities life grants us. Worse, we may overlook our own potential to create limitless possibilities. That reflection was the beginning of this book. I just didn't know it at the time.

The Last Lecture

In 2007, Dr. Randy F. Pausch, a professor of computer sciences at Carnegie Mellon University, was diagnosed with pancreatic cancer and told he had three to six months to live. Wanting to make the most of that time, he left his job and moved his family somewhere they could focus on being together. Before he left Carnegie Mellon, he gave one last lecture, which the university posted online. To date, the original video has more than twenty million views. The news media, including Oprah Winfrey, shared the lecture and Randy's story. Eventually, *The Last Lecture* became a best-selling book.

Why did this lecture make such a splash? Pausch spoke about achieving his childhood dreams and his experiences and lessons about life. His goal wasn't to impact millions; it was to pass on all the wisdom he could to his young children.

His last lecture told them of his legacy—his life well lived.

I don't know about you, but I don't want to wait until I'm dead or dying to share my legacy. I want to make an impact on the world now—with my life as much as with my words. Instead of waiting until the end of my life to deliver a "Last Lecture" or making them figure it out on their own, I have determined to tell my kids, "Look, this is what matters to me and what I am about. This is what we're experiencing together as a family and what I hope you can create and experience in your own lives." I am also intentional about demonstrating those lessons by the way I live my life *now* and the values I stand for and focus my life around.

Part of my legacy is this book and the lessons and principles within—or what I call *Lifetime Expanders*™. This book is *my* first lecture. What you learn will equip you to choose what you want for *your* legacy so you can write *your* first lecture.

Are You Living a *Great* Life?

I am a Visionary, an entrepreneur, a leader, a husband, a dad, and a coach—Coach Bob. My driving force in life is to elevate the entrepreneurial spirit through self-mastery and connection—ultimately to help people know *and* act like they matter. We created the iMatter Journey specifically to help people transform their lives, take control of their destinies, and step into their greatness. That is my North Star (something we'll discuss later). I've built my career around this calling, and my greatest desire is that my legacy is one of example. I want not only to teach the iMatter Journey but also to live it out every day.

If you're like many of my coaching clients, some areas of your life are clicking along pretty well. Life is good, but you feel like something is missing. You want more than a *good* life; you want an energizing, joyful, meaningful, *great* life.

If you're not experiencing freedom, joy, and peace, chances are you are aware of the gap between the life of your dreams and the reality of now.

Perhaps you hear the nagging voice of doubt or constant negative chatter in your head: *Am I successful? Am I a great father or mother or grandparent or sibling? Am I making a huge difference? What happened to the magic of childhood? Do I matter?*

Perhaps you feel scattered and overwhelmed by the have-tos—the responsibilities that keep you busy and leave you feeling like you have little control over your time and energy.

Perhaps there are so many things you want to do *someday*—if only you had the time.

Perhaps you're constantly striving for—but never attaining—success because your goal is measuring up to someone else or an arbitrary number in your bank account, and the target changes constantly.

The iMatter Journey is about tapping into the wisdom of the ages to give you the power to be exponentially *you*. I hope that by the time you get to the end of this book, you will realize you do indeed matter, and the answers that will guide you to the life you want are inside *you*. As you discover what is truly important to you and muster the courage and confidence to be who *you* are, you will flip those "Am I" questions into "I Am" statements of certainty. In short, you will know deep inside your heart and soul the feeling of iMatter.

Before We Begin

Like any great journey, life's path hasn't always been easy for me. I am grateful for the challenges, though, because they have helped me become who I am today. It gives me great pleasure, now, to serve as an experienced guide for others—people like you—who are on the adventure of their life.

Before you and I set out on this trek together, I want to provide you with a little backstory so you can understand how and why we developed the principles, practices, and tools that comprise the iMatter Journey. I share my story openly and honestly because I want you to see how using the iMatter Journey as my personal operating system transformed my life. I am not offended, though, if you prefer to jump ahead to the next chapter and dive into your own iMatter journey.

Questioning My Destiny

I had been working for a company that dominated the international mail distribution industry when I discovered some unseemly practices going on. A colleague and I planned to start a company of our own. On the morning of our first big meeting to land our anchor account, my colleague called to tell me that the company (the one we just left) had asked him to stay. They'd made him an offer that he couldn't refuse. They'd even told him they wanted me to stay, too, and would give me a raise. The offer was flattering—and tempting. I had to stop and think about what really mattered to me.

I left and opened Great White North Distribution Services in Chicago in 1993. (If you're a fan of the classic 80's comedy *Strange Brew*, you may appreciate the name.) My company catered to a specific niche, which, combined with our simplified process, integrity, and dedicated customer service, put us on an incredible growth trajectory of 5,000 percent in five years. The company earned the #26 spot on *Inc.*'s list of the 500 fastest-growing privately held companies.

A Wake-Up Call from the Universe

During those five years of exceptional business growth, it seemed as if I could succeed at anything. In reality, I was coasting. The universe has a funny way of shaking us out of our stupor when we least expect it.

In May of 1995, I was in Denver to visit an important client. One morning, looking out the twenty-third-floor window of the Westin Hotel, I saw a rainbow arc over the peaks of the Rockies. I took it as a good omen: My company was growing, business was booming, and here I was about to build on that success. I felt destined for greatness.

The next morning, I was driving seventy-five miles per hour heading south on I-25 in a rented Ford Taurus. Rain poured down in surreal, greenish sheets, and I remember thinking that I had plenty of time to get to my meeting, so I should just slow down and enjoy the drive. I eased my foot off the accelerator, dropping to sixty.

Without warning, a car flew across the median and slammed into me head-on. It happened so fast I didn't have time to get the curse word out of my mouth.

As I lay in the wreckage, I heard the soft hissing noises emanating from the crumpled cars. The harsh smell of the blasted airbag gunpowder burned my nostrils. I looked down next to me and noticed with dismay that my briefcase and cell phone were smashed to bits. Wondering whether I was dying, I thought, *Not now. Things are just starting to go well.*

Then a beautiful blonde woman came up to what used to be the window, dressed in a flowing white chiffon dress. Looking at her bare feet, I worried that she would cut her feet on the broken glass that surrounded the car. Before I could warn her to be careful, she told me I would be all right and not to worry because God was with me. A moment later, she was gone.

The paramedics arrived. I struggled for breath as they removed me from the car and put me in an ambulance. I asked the EMT, "Where's the woman with the bare feet?" I wanted them to find her and bandage her up. I hadn't seen her coming when she suddenly appeared at my window, so I assumed she had walked up from behind me. I asked them to check the cars that had been backed-up by the accident. My rescuers did so but couldn't find the woman anywhere and told me no one else had seen her.

I have no way of knowing whether the woman was a human being, a dream, or a benevolent spirit, but I'm sure she was an angel. She distracted me from my pain and gave me something to hold on to. I felt like George Bailey in *It's a Wonderful Life*. Her presence sparked a newfound awareness within me—an awareness that there was more to life than I had thought and that I was on this earth for a greater purpose.

I can only hope that she visited the guy in the other car, too.

Through that experience, the universe brought me in touch with my own mortality. After waking up to the fact that my life could be taken from me at any moment, I realized there was more to it than earning a good living. A nice home was great, but there had to be more significance to my existence.

Not long after that car wreck, my twenty-three-year-old brother-in-law suddenly passed away from a pulmonary embolism. He had spent the day with his fiancé, planning their wedding. Then he went to sleep and never woke up.

Have you ever experienced a moment that compelled you to question everything about your existence?

The mass of people who showed up for this young man's funeral awed me. Many of them had only met him one time, but his sincerity and genuine love for people touched the lives of everyone around him. Looking at the crowd, I couldn't help but wonder who would show up to my funeral. *What would they say about me in the eulogy?*

At that time, I worried the answer was that most people would show up out of obligation. People would say I was a hard worker, funny, driven, a good guy—but few would know the real me. *What legacy would I leave?* I suddenly felt empty.

I had achieved or acquired almost everything I thought mattered. I lived in a beautifully furnished dream house. I had season tickets for all the local sports teams. I had a beautiful wife and was running my own business. In truth, however, I had spent years coasting along without a greater sense of purpose. I had done and acquired those things mostly because that's what I thought success was supposed to look like. My life, up to that point, wasn't enough to leave a mark on the world.

From the outside, I had it made. Inside, however, I felt an overwhelming sense of sadness. I couldn't help but question why I was here, what my purpose was, and what mattered most—to me. Sitting at my brother-in-law's funeral, I thought, *When it is time for me to go, I want to leave this world knowing that I've fulfilled my destiny to make a huge difference in the world and lived a legacy I am proud of.*

The problem? I had no idea what my destiny was or what my legacy would be. Adding to my confusion was the fact that my business had fallen on hard times. We had turned down a merger offer and were working long hours trying to make up for cash shortfalls. My struggling marriage had started to unravel.

One day during a meeting with my EO forum group, I confided, "Guys, I feel like a failure. My company is a financial mess, my marriage is in trouble, and I don't know who I am."

When you make an admission like that to a group of entrepreneurial go-getters, you might expect to receive a tough, drill-sergeant lecture about keeping a stiff upper lip—or worse, the uncomfortable silence of rejection. Instead, one of the guys answered, "We know. What are we going to do about it?"

What I thought I had been hiding so well was obvious to many others but not me. My forum brothers put aside all judgment and helped me tackle my problems. The vulnerability I had shown inspired others to admit that their lives weren't what they wanted them to be either. Suddenly it seemed like we were all asking the same question: *What matters most—to me?*

Something shifted inside me. In the past, I'd had people tell me I was a terrible businessperson because I didn't have a knack for details and wasn't a good manager. I had taken those words to heart and learned to doubt myself. Through the conversations with my EO group and after some personal reflection, I looked at life in a new way. I started to turn my life around and recognize my value as a business leader and as a person.

Soon after, I met Gino Wickman and discovered what later became EOS®, the Entrepreneurial Operating System®. Gino not only became a great friend, confidante, and coach for me but also validated my leadership style and gave me a name for it: Visionary.

I learned that my style of leadership worked best when I used my Visionary traits to their advantage and tapped into others' abilities to manage the details. EOS taught me the value of structure and a process. Using those tools, my team and I were able to define who we are as a company and where we are going.

At this time, I also learned about creating my reality by establishing goals, believing in them, and putting positive energy out into the universe. Exercising the power of faith, my team evaluated our situation and realized we could focus on the pain of our present circumstances, or we could choose to believe in our future success and build toward it. With absolutely nothing to lose, we launched a major culture-change initiative in the middle of our cash crisis.

Long story short: It worked. By putting the right people in the right places, playing to our strengths, and connecting to our core values, the company recovered, and soon, we were hitting our goals quarter after quarter.

Figuring Myself Out

Despite the business's turnaround, I knew leading that company wasn't my destiny or part of the legacy I wanted to leave, at least not all of it. Eventually, I determined I needed to figure myself out. I put my team in charge of the business and took several months off. I traveled to Colorado, climbed mountains, met healers and shamans, and began to connect with my true self—who I was, what kind of life I wanted, and what mattered most to me. It was during this time of solitude and reflection that I made the tough decision to separate from my wife. I rented a cabin on a lake. Being alone gave me time to connect with myself, someone I was just getting to know.

This was a difficult period in my life. To outward appearances, I was dismantling a perfectly good life and going through an intense midlife crisis. What looked like a breakdown to others was actually a breakthrough. For the first time in my life, I stopped to think about what I wanted and what was important to me. With the clarity I gained in the quietness of that cabin, I made decisions with the belief that *I mattered*—my needs, my soul's desires, my hopes, dreams, destiny, and legacy *mattered*.

One key insight from that time was the degree to which external stress had been ruining my life. I recalled how, several Christmases before, I had begrudged the time my family required of me wondering, *How can these people be having fun? I'm wasting time here on a bunch of nonsense!*

Christmas should have been a time of peace, love, and slowing down. Instead, stress, outside pressures, and my business constantly consumed my thoughts, ruining Christmas for me and everyone around me.

In the quiet of the cabin, I realized I needed to live in the moment if I was going to experience peace in my life. At that point, I determined not to allow stress or society's illusory demands take me down and stop me from living.

I sold my remaining interest in my business. After briefly running a small software company, I set myself free to invest all my energies into my personal journey and lead and inspire others on their journeys. I enjoyed learning new self-growth and discovery strategies and adding value to people's lives by teaching them what I had learned. I stepped into my next phase of life and became Coach Bob. I began working with entrepreneurs and executives to help them shift their thinking, dive into their souls, and find more meaning and magic in their lives. It was both cool and scary to vulnerably share with clients what I was learning and experiencing in my own life and business. As I ran into and overcame obstacles, I shared my process for solving problems. We then used those processes to address the challenges they faced.

Every step of the journey led to the message and truth of that, whoever you are, you mattered. It was essential, I discovered, that each person, including myself, had to affirm that truth: I matter.

Through trial and error, I found clarity about my life's true purpose, and I embraced my coaching calling and started iMatter, which is the mindset, the mantra, the movement for getting in touch with your spirit and melding your belief system with your actions. I have since worked with many leaders, entrepreneurs, and other visionaries, equipping them with the message and the tools of the iMatter Journey so they, too, can shift their mindset and choose to live meaningful lives filled with purpose and passion. The people I've worked with have found peace, freedom, joy, love, and truth in living out what matters most to them. They know and act like they matter. We call this recognition of innate personal value *stepping into greatness* or *self-mastery*.

My goal, the legacy I want to leave, is a revolution: the iMatter Revolution.

In starting my coaching and training business, I intentionally designed my work and schedule. I didn't want to lose myself in my work as I had previously. Instead, I chose to be in the moment. I used rituals to guide me daily so I could grow toward and expand the life I wanted. I took time each week to reflect on and celebrate my progress. And as my new life took shape, so did my thinking about how each person can succeed at business *and* live a great life.

My journey of self-mastery began twenty-five years ago and continues each and every day to be an adventure. Since that time, I married a smart, beautiful woman, Sheryl (we recently celebrated our twenty-second anniversary), and we are blessed with two amazing children, Grace and Nick, as well as an awesome dog, Brady. Grace has known who she is since she was young and has been an example of integrity and being of service. She has the courage to create spiritual conversations. Nick taught us when he was young that love is magic, and magic is God. He has been a shining example of continuously flipping a negative situation into a positive. My wife has been an integral part of helping me shift my paradigms about life and living and helping me learn to be. She is my partner not only in life but also in the development of creating iMatter, the writing of this book, and implementing the iMatter Journey in our lives. She and I are soulmates and on a path to bring iMatter and to create a place to BE in communities one soul at a time. (Visit APlaceToBe.com to learn more.)

With iMatter, you don't have to coast along and wait for a car to come crashing over the median. You can take charge of your legacy right *now*!

PART 1

The Time Is *Now* for iMatter

1

The Time Is Now

I t is a crazy time to be alive.

In the past few years, we have experienced a world-wide pandemic, foreign and domestic political upheaval, crippling fear and limitation, economic shutdowns, and riots in the streets.

We've also experienced some of the greatest break-throughs in technology and science. We've seen amazing acts of love and human kindness and have experienced incredible moments of connection on a global scale.

Yeah, it's a crazy time to be alive. It is up to you, however, to decide whether *crazy* means good or bad—or something else altogether. Likewise, you're faced with deciding whether *crazy* means life is completely out of your grasp—or completely within your control.

What you *choose* to believe is based on your thoughts and often on your mindset. I've observed and coached so many people who are looking outside themselves to get where they want to be or to feel successful. Seeking external cues is our culture's default setting. If my journey has helped me realize anything, it's that your truth is not revealed through outward observation but through *inward experience*. This paradigm shift was a game changer for me. *Thinking* differently helped me to *act* and *be* differently in my life as I came home to myself and that inner faith and knowing that *iMatter*.

The process of Think–Act–Be™, was born from this realization and helped me *view* and *do* my life differently. This process is the core of the iMatter Journey. It calls me—and you—to slow down, discern between scattered mental chatter and the soul's true calling, and commit to stepping into greatness.

The clarity that came from using Think-Act-Be (a key process of iMatter) caused *success* to take on a whole new meaning for me.

Redefining Success

For a long time, I measured success in dollars or in what some people call "ringing the bell" (for the group I was hanging with, it was $10 million in the bank for selling our business). When I stopped comparing myself to others, I realized that success is *not* defined by wealth, possessions, or societal pressure. It took time and effort to finally accept I could define success for myself.

I invite you to do the same.

Success, to me, has to do with what feeds my spirit: the love of my family, faith in my children and the thrill of supporting their growth, and the ability to find joy in everyday moments, like the warm sun on my head or the grass beneath my feet.

When I redefined success for myself, I understood that it didn't matter whether others had bigger houses or more money. What they're experiencing is not what matters most *to me*. I know that appearances can be deceiving and that all those things don't equate to true success.

Letting go of my past ideas about success freed me to *be* in the world in new ways and see it with fresh eyes. Realizing what matters most *to me*, clarifying and being who I am, and following my North Star helped me tap into my personal definition of success, which is being present, open-minded, energized, in love, and experiencing joy!

I feel fortunate to be a Visionary (a hard thing to say because I used to think I was a bit of an outlier). Part of my purpose and passion in life is to use my vision to help open the door for others and inspire them to access their inner wisdom and step into their greatness. I have found that when our lives are in turmoil, the spirit is what carries us through. Tapping into my spirit, looking inward, is what ultimately helped me define success and step into my own greatness.

I believe every human being matters to the world and that we can all live our best lives with a sense of meaning and deep satisfaction. These can be tricky thoughts to embrace fully, but we're poised to do so *now* like never before. Reviving belief (or perhaps finding it for the first time) requires a great deal of mental work because of the heavy load of spiritual and emotional baggage over the ages, not just as individuals but as a society. One generation feeds the next on the wisdom it has adopted.

I like to explain why the time is now for amazing break-throughs by looking at how communication has changed over time, how thoughts have been shared and paradigms formed. New technologies open new possibilities for exchanging information and wisdom exponentially. This amazing time of transition as a society allows us to advance into the next age and tap into our inner wisdom.

WELCOME TO THE WISDOM AGE™

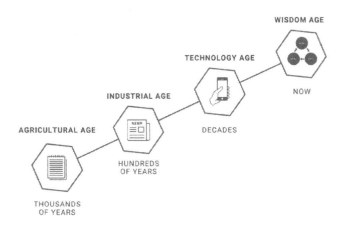

The Agricultural Age (1-to-1 Communication)

The agricultural age was the beginning of human civili-zation, and it lasted for thousands of years. People shared wisdom, thoughts, questions, and experiences primarily in one-to-one conversations. I would speak with you, you would speak to your spouse, and so on. I'd write a note to you; you might write a letter to a relative a few states over. This was the age of the Socratic dialogue.

Industrial Age (1-to-Many Communication)

The industrial age was led by entrepreneurs, and the mode of communication was impacted drastically by the invention of the printing press. Suddenly, we were communicating one-to-many. An individual could create a book, newspaper, or flyer and distribute it to thousands of people. Whereas before, ideas about philosophy, politics, and spirit were disseminated from a king or priest, now they could circulate horizontally amongst communities. People could ask great questions and question the status quo in open dialogue.

The Technology Age (Many-to-Many, Instant Communication)

The invention of the computer and the internet issued in the Technology Age. With the growth of the internet, I can put out information to millions of people, and I can get millions of bits of information back. As exciting as it is, it's easy to get lost in all that information and miss that one-to-one intimacy. The technology age misled us into the idea that it was perfectly acceptable to seek immediate gratification—and that our devices were going to solve all our problems. In reality, our devices started insisting that everything was urgent, and we became overwhelmed with the outside chatter.

Welcome to the Wisdom Age (Internal Communication and Being)

The next frontier isn't in outer space; it is inside each and every one of us. It's about what we can discover in ourselves, the untapped potential and life force we suppress because of fear or the desire to conform.

As I considered the shift from the Technology Age to the Wisdom Age, I had to ask: *What if we started believing in our inner wisdom, our inner genius?*

Years ago, I watched the last astronaut-occupied space shuttle take off from Kennedy Space Center in Florida. It may have been a trick of the light or my mind, but the exhaust lit up red, white, and blue, and as the aura faded away, I felt sad, thinking that was the end of space as the next frontier.

Space exploration ushered in a new period of innovation and discovery and was a great example of people and governments coming together and rallying in the same direction. It was a very external example of what people can accomplish when they put their minds together.

I've heard our age called the Exponential Age and a few other things, but I call it the Wisdom Age. What does that mean? It means that, although we can find infinite amounts of knowledge *out there*, at the end of the day, we have an unprecedented opportunity to grow in *wisdom* within.

The value of this age is not about what is *outside* of me. The value of this age comes from tapping into the wisdom *inside* me, inside *you*, and sharing to learn, grow and expand together. It's very intimate, and it's a revolution that we're all a part of. The Wisdom Age offers many tools for breaking out of our default settings and our old paradigms; almost anyone can become a guru or thought leader or just *be* themselves—whatever that means to them.

As we find and rely on our inner wisdom and genius, we realize we have all the answers inside us. *We matter*, we just need to remember to stop and shift our mindset, find that wisdom within and then share it with others as part of our continued learning process. To stay solely within our minds is to subject ourselves to our pond of stagnation, to the old ideas of the ages we have internalized, to the rules our parents preached, the negative views we have learned from unsupportive people, and our undesirable habits or what we call in this book: the chatter. Unscattering the chatter and stepping into our greatness through self-mastery is what this new age (and this book) is all about: to show up, share our wisdom with one another, and be present in life from that harmony and deep knowing that each person matters.

One of my core beliefs is that *this is the greatest time to be alive*. If we don't think that our future is greater than our past, we shrink back instead of stepping forward into our greatness. Evolution is revolution, my friend.

Yes, digital technology gives us access to information, but the best technology for this age is an ancient one: dialogue. MIT professor Dr. Bill Isaacs, whom I was fortunate enough to study with years ago, liked to say, "Dialogue is the art of learning together." I have my experiences and opinions, and you have yours. As we share our thoughts and ideas, we may or may not convince one another to change our beliefs, but wisdom is all about learning *together*. When we share our experiences with others, we learn. The acts of speaking and listening reveal the wisdom within.

The more we share our experience with others, the more we improve our chances of understanding this new frontier. We bring

> "Your greatness is here and now.
> Your happiness is here and now."
>
> —Napoleon Hill

the many-to-many back to the one-to-one communication. Our ability to make an impact on any number of people at any given moment by sharing truth is an amazing gift.

Despite all that's going on outside of us in the world, I believe it's an extraordinary time to be alive. I'm excited to be a part of the journey of enlightenment we are on together. I hope you're excited and ready to jump into becoming the greatest version of yourself. The time is *now*.

Welcome to the Wisdom Age!

2

Are You Ready?

This book is not for people who want to spend the rest of their life gathering wisdom and researching life skills but never applying them. It is not for those averse to diving deep and choosing a greater life. It is not for people who want to stay stuck, stressed, and burnt out or spinning their wheels and never feeling like they get anywhere.

This book is for you if and when you decide you are ready to say, "I matter."

Knowing and feeling like *you* matter is a lifelong journey. Clients have told me the iMatter Journey is "a structured way, to find your way" and that "the journey is a path to freedom, joy, and peace." The good news is that *you* get to decide what your journey will be.

> "Once you make a decision, the universe conspires to make it happen."
>
> —Ralph Waldo Emerson

I've organized this book to equip you to align with your true self and focus on what matters most to you. Using the principles and tools you find here will empower you to create the life you desire. Be forewarned, though: It takes discipline to install a whole new operating system—a way to view and live your life. The word *discipline* often gets a bad rap because people assume it means doing things you don't want to do. My argument is that when it comes to what matters most, discipline can be about investing in yourself rather than devoting all your time and energy to external demands or struggles. In fact, discipline can be the greatest form of self-love.

What does *self-love* mean? If I believe in myself and love myself, I know that I have a lot to offer and put out into the world. By being disciplined, I can do the things that matter most. I can make choices that will further my goals and sustain me. I focus on "what I *choose* to do" rather than "what I *have* to do."

Exercise is a simple example of self-love. I don't *have* to exercise every week. I *choose* to exercise because being healthy matters to me. Having this type of discipline in my life ensures that I take precious time for myself. It means I am taking care of my mind, body, and spirit. Without discipline, these scales can tip and remain unbalanced and unchecked.

It's up to you to decide what and who matters to you and then to arrange your life accordingly. To flip your perception of discipline and view it as an act of self-love, shift your focus to creating rituals, habits, and practices that sustain you and push you closer to your definition of success. Evaluate the things in your life that also do the opposite.

The discipline of adopting and practicing the iMatter tools and strategies—your new operating system—will require intentionality, but the rewards will be worth the effort.

Prepare for a System Reboot

Before you can install a new operating system, you're going to need to make space for it. When your computer or smartphone needs an update, it uninstalls the existing operating system before uploading the new files. In the same way, think of this initial phase as debugging or uninstalling a faulty or out-of-date system.

We'll begin by uninstalling the habits and thoughts—mindsets—that are holding you back. You will be shifting your mindset using the iMatter principles. You'll learn how to let go of old paradigms and preconceived notions, drop your own and others' expectations and biases, and release yourself from the weight of mental and emotional baggage. In other words, you'll clear out the chatter that keeps leading you back to the place of doubt and disappointment.

Without those old habits and hang-ups cluttering your mind, you'll be free to explore life with curiosity, joy, and hope. Like a brand-new computer, you will have plenty of mental space to hold and run with new ideas. Installing this life-success system will guide you toward a new way of thinking, acting, and being in your life.

To gauge your readiness for the journey to becoming the next greatest version of *you*, ask yourself these questions:

- Am I ready to move from having a *good* life to having a *great* life?
- Am I ready to *imagine* an amazing future, *improve* on my past successes and failures, and truly *impact* my life destiny?
- Am I ready to let go of unhealthy chatter or the beliefs, behaviors, and habits that are holding me back from stepping into my greatness?

- Am I ready to let my spirit guide me to realize what matters most (my what), clarify who I am and my Great Gift™ (my how), and follow my North Star (my why) in life?
- Am I ready to create from my full potential and design a legacy that brings me joy while also serving and inspiring others?
- Am I ready to live and act like *iMatter*?

The time is *now*. Don't wait for a cancer diagnosis, heart attack or stroke, divorce, or an empty nest to start living a meaningful life. You can start living the life of your dreams right here, right now, with this book in your hands if you so choose.

You can begin right now. Start changing your mindset by saying the following sentences aloud:

I am open and evolving.
I am on a journey of self-mastery.
I am stepping into my greatness.

PART 2

Shift Your Mindset

3

What Is iMatter?

'Ve packed all the wisdom I have to offer you into iMatter, starting with the name. It stands for both the process and the outcome. A key insight of iMatter is that happiness and joy come from *within* you, not from what you *do* or *acquire*. The affirmation, "I matter," is both the origin and the goal. It begins with the acknowledgment, "I matter enough not to go chasing some other person's idea of success but to find happiness and joy in my own life and in what success means to me." The affirmation continues as a journey of enlightenment that helps you *be* who you are and experience peace, joy, and freedom. You will discover your true self as you elevate your mindset and let go of old paradigms. As you do that, you will be able to clarify who you are and focus on what matters most to you. From there, you are free to step into your greatness, follow your North Star, and expand your impact to the people around you.

iMatter is a mindset. It's a mantra. It's a revolution.

It's a personal journey for living a magnificent, meaningful, and magical life.

And it starts with *you*!

Shifting to Believing iMatter

Before I could shift my mindset and choose to step into my greatness, I needed to realize that my life, my destiny, and my legacy were worth pursuing. I had to believe that *I mattered*. As I mentioned in the previous chapter, for years, I had pursued success by society's standards, basing my happiness on how I compared to others, the wealth of my possessions, and how much money was in my bank account.

By society's standards, I was doing pretty well, but honestly, I didn't feel all that successful. The reason? I was pursuing and measuring the wrong things.

Society teaches us to separate the spiritual from the material. Self-care, family, and fun, for example, are kept apart from work and financial success. This division between *being* and *doing* creates constant tension as we teeter between the two.

In contrast, the iMatter mindset puts a combined emphasis on both the *I* (which we sometimes call the spiritual) *and* the *matter* (the stuff of everyday life). The resulting belief is that iMatter to the world and am happiest when I define success for myself and live in that reality and that harmony of the *and*.

My life began to change when I came to understand that balance and harmony between the spiritual and the material was not only attainable but essential.

To be honest, it wasn't easy for me to make the initial shifts in my own mindset—even though I desperately needed to change. Like many, I suffered disappointment and felt fed up and frustrated with my life. I also felt confused. I wanted a more meaningful life, but I didn't know how to change my circumstances or my thinking because I didn't have the right tools or mindset . . . yet.

Change Your Thinking, Change Your Life

If you feel stuck or unsure about your life or what success means to you, you have some work to do before you can begin living by the principles and harnessing the power of the tools in the iMatter Journey. You'll need to reset your mindset—beliefs about yourself and your life—or reboot your system. Then you will be able to make a commitment to yourself that you matter.

The iMatter mindset recognizes and builds upon who you are—your true self, your *whole* self. Your new mindset bridges the "I," the spiritual side, where love, faith, belief, creativity, magic, and the other intangibles of "being" reside, and "matter," the material side, which consists of your physical needs, your financial wealth, the goods you own, your business or career, as well as your intellect, reason, desires, and fears.

iMATTER

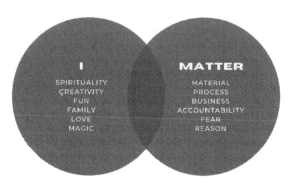

I
SPIRITUALITY
CREATIVITY
FUN
FAMILY
LOVE
MAGIC

MATTER
MATERIAL
PROCESS
BUSINESS
ACCOUNTABILITY
FEAR
REASON

A BRIDGE BETWEEN SPIRITUAL AND MATERIAL

When you develop the foundational belief that your whole self matters and bridge the spiritual and the material, you will discover the joy and abundance of the *and* rather than suffer the tyranny of the *or*.

The truth is, it's difficult (if not impossible) to be happy living from a this-*or*-that mindset. If you have to choose between your career or your family, you lose. If you have to choose between fun or work, you lose. If you have to choose between wellness or financial success, you lose.

Or doesn't work.

When you live in the abundance of *and*, you don't have to choose between your professional and personal life because you find the balance where both can exist in harmony.

> **If you have to choose between fun or work, you lose. If you have to choose between wellness or financial success, you lose. *Or* doesn't work.**

Once I discovered *I mattered*, I began to understand the importance of being myself in both the *I* world and the *matter* world. I've learned not to worry about what other people think. I stopped trying to act the way I thought they wanted me to act. Instead, I am unapologetically myself regardless of who is around, and I rest in the knowledge that is enough. I am me—iM!

In fact, we have coined the term iM™. This is when the I and matter come together in life as one in the harmony of the *and* or iM (the power of I am)!

THE iMATTER MINDSET™

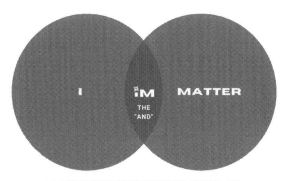

I AND MATTER COME TOGETHER AS ONE = IM
HARMONY OF THE "AND" OR SELF-MASTERY

I have found that when the *I* and the *matter* are one, I feel freedom and can be present in the moment, be in love, and be at peace. This is true self-mastery to me (living in the harmony of the *and* or iM). My choices and path become clearer in life. The work or craft I'm meant to do and my purpose in the world unfold easily in my life because I'm fulfilling my passion; it enriches my soul as well as my bank account because I am impacting the moment as my exponential self. I love life. I have fun. I contribute to the world, and the world rewards me for it.

This may sound too simple and thus too easy. If it were easy, everyone would have a wonderful, happy, great life. The problem is, taking good care of oneself can be a lot of work and often requires overcoming some doubts. The iMatter Journey is a deep dive into how you view and do your life. It's about observing how you are thinking, speaking, and reacting in your day-to-day. Often people find they "react" to situations based on past belief systems or fears. As you go through this journey with an open mind and open heart and examine your life further, you will discover it's possible to let go of living in limitation and shift how you show up and speak your truth into the world. It takes intentionality to take care of and listen to your body and soul. It takes mindfulness to weed out negative thoughts and bad habits and replace them with constructive thinking.

As you elevate your mind, you have the ability to become the observer of your thoughts and actions and not get caught up in your emotions. By taking the reactions, habits, and baggage out of the equation, you can witness the opportunities to learn, grow, and expand. As the observer, you realize you are *not* your thoughts. You have a choice. Shift your *thinking*, and you change how you are *acting* and *being* in your life (Think-Act-Be). I've found that it's up to me to consistently choose happiness and make an effort to harvest the fruits of my labors. That is why I created the iMatter Journey. It is a journey that takes you into yourself and builds and expands outward so you can create harmony in your life and live in the power of iM!

The Power of iM

It turns out that the number seven in numerology is about the spirit and accessing inner wisdom. It is also a combination of three and four together. Three is creativity, and four is practicality. The "I" and the "matter" come together to reach seven, a highly spiritual number associated with mysticism and intuition (iMatter). In the Bible, seven is considered the most powerful and lucky number in Scripture. In fact, seven refers to the creation of the world, accomplished in seven days according to Genesis. Furthermore, the seventh card in a tarot deck is the Chariot. It is about a quest, using both intention and focus to drive energy toward purpose.

This quest is what the iMatter Journey is all about. Using Think-Act-Be, the journey takes you on an exploration of your spirit and inner wisdom. Anchoring yourself with the principles or lessons using the *seven* Lifetime Expanders—tools to focus and drive your energy toward your purpose and your truth—you will step into your greatness, expand into self-mastery (shifting from Am I? to I Am), and know the power of iM!

4

The Think-Act-Be Process

How often have you said or thought something like this?

As soon as I have more money, I can do this thing I always wanted to do or get this thing I always wanted to have, and then I'll finally be happy.

How has that worked out for you so far?

If you are like most high achievers and entrepreneurs, you end up working eighty hours a week, always striving for the next project, the next deal, the next goal. Your family hardly sees you, and when they do, you are on your mobile device answering emails and responding to one urgent message after another. Sure, you may take a few days off each year for a vacation, but what about the rest of your life?

In the last chapter, we looked at the tension created by trying to live by the mindset society forces on us that separates *I* (spiritual) from *matter* (material). That same tension shows up in this Western cultural concept of "I'll be happy when I have or achieve _____." (I'll let you fill in that blank for yourself.) We strive and push and claw to reach the goal, but the happiness? If it comes at all, it's fleeting because we're already on to the next project and never really *living* or *being* in the moment.

But what if you redefined success as working toward a goal *and* enjoying your life on a daily basis? (Remember, the goal is *and* not *or*.) What if you chose to *be* in the moment right now, see the beauty of life unfolding, and then *act* from that place of contentment? What might you *have* then?

Our default Western mindset regarding success is Have–Do–Be. If I *have* this and that (usually, more money or things money can buy), then I can *do* the things I want, and I'll finally *be* happy, *be* in love, and *be* present in the moment.

HAVE-DO-BE

Unfortunately, this mentality usually leads to a lot of unhappiness and anxiety. That's because its focus is on the externals, on what you have or accumulate, rather than on what really matters. But remember, one of the core truths of the iMatter mindset is that happiness comes from *within* you, not from the things you *do* or *acquire*.

This Have–Do–Be mindset also thrives on comparisons: What does my neighbor have? My coworker? My Facebook friends? As famously quoted, "Comparison is the thief of joy." When you look to see how you measure up, you'll always find people with more money than you, nicer clothes, more exciting vacations, and more education. No matter how much more you acquire, it will never be enough if you are basing your happiness on comparisons.

Our society's Have–Do–Be mindset leads to, at best, *conditional happiness* because all of these external things are temporary and out of your control.

Be–Do–Have

Be–Do–Have is an ancient Eastern mindset that flips the script on our more modern Western approach of Have–Do–Be.

Neale Donald Walsch writes about this in his third *Conversations with God* book. He calls it the "Be–Do–Have Paradigm":

> Most people believe if they "have" a thing (more time, money, love—whatever), then they can finally "do" a thing (write a book, take up a hobby, go on vacation, buy a home, undertake a relationship), which will allow them to "be" a thing (happy, peaceful, content, in the moment, or in love).
>
> In actuality, they are reversing the Be–Do–Have paradigm. In the universe as it is (as opposed to how you think it is), "havingness" does not produce "beingness," but the other way around.

Walsch argues that the real order of the universe requires us to first be present in our lives in the moment. (We can't live in the past or future, anyhow; we only have the present.) If we can *be* ourselves, we can *do* things from a position of integrity and strength—and guess what? In the being and doing, we discover we already *have* everything we need.

Much of the time, in living out of this Be–Do–Have mindset, we may even discover that what we thought we wanted wasn't really what mattered most but a symbol of something deeper; for example, a lavish vacation would be nice to have, but what we really want is more quality time with our families and some much-needed rest.

If you believe the *have* will follow the *be* and the *do*, you're right. And if you're thinking, *Bullshit, Bob,* you're right about that, too, because you're coming at life from an ineffective mindset.

Reverse your assumption. *Be* in the moment. *Do* the next right thing. You will discover that you either already *have* what you need or what you need shows up at just the right time. We can never *have* our way into *being*. We must lead with spirituality, an open heart, and let our soul guide us.

> **We can never *have* our way into *being*. We must lead with spirituality, an open heart, and let our soul guide us.**

Think-Act-Be

The iMatter mindset prompts the universal process of Be–Do–Have into reality with the precursor principle of Think-Act-Be.

THINK-ACT-BE™

When my wife, Sheryl, and I learned the universal truth of the Be–Do–Have process some twenty years ago, we were so excited because it worked! We were learning to be in the moment. Of course, it worked! It was a magical moment of transformation in which we were literally standing on top of a mountain without a care in the world. Full of revelation and confidence, we reveled in the moment and shouted, "We've got it!"

To which the universe responded, "Okay, let's see if you really have it."

Fast-forward a few years to when we were new parents, and our businesses were struggling. We were under a lot of stress, and suddenly it wasn't so easy to be in the moment. Life had gone off the rails. How were we going to get back on track?

Returning to what we knew to be true and what we believed mattered most, we developed a process to answer that desperate question: change your thinking, change your actions, and *then* be who you are. In other words, Think-Act-Be. We quickly identified Think-Act-Be as a key process in the iMatter mindset. It is key to tap into the mindset of Be–Do–Have when life is doing its damnedest to keep you stuck and striving in Have–Do–Be mode.

Here's the basic idea: Even when I'm totally caught up in all the things that seem so urgent, I can usually stop for a moment to *think*. I can ask myself a question like, *Why am I struggling with _____?* Or *Am I a good Visionary?* Starting from a place of mindful self-reflection, I can unearth what's going on in my head and my heart. I then make time to write down my response and share my thoughts with trusted friends, my spouse, or a mentor to shift the conversation in my head, unscatter the chatter, clarify who I am, and realize what matters most to me.

As I begin to elevate my mind and realize the chatter doesn't control me, I can start to *act* on the things that matter most to me at that time. I can *choose* to stay in the present, impact the current moment, and *act* like iMatter.

From there, I arrive at *being*—the gates of this universal process of Be–Do–Have. Then I'm back to honoring what matters most to me and following my North Star. When I know iMatter and live from the space of this harmony as who iM, that is true self-mastery.

THE iMATTER PROCESS™

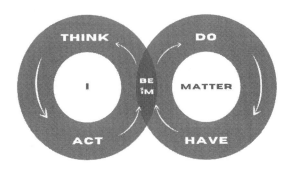

CENTER = IM - HARMONY - BE SPACE

Think-Act-Be is foundational to the iMatter Journey, helping you harness the power of the iMatter mindset and supporting you in your intention to live a *great* life. Anytime fear, doubt, or uncertainty about your next step fills your mind with chatter, stop and Think–Act–Be. This, along with the other tools in the iMatter Journey, will enable you to get out of your own way, begin again, and choose to take the next right step on your adventure of life.

As proof that using this process continues to help me expand and evolve, I will often share my own experience in my journey of self-mastery in this book. You've read a lot of my story already, so you know that I've been developing, practicing, and refining the principles, practices, and tools of the iMatter Journey for almost twenty-five years. The truth is, I am *still* defining and refining or rebooting and installing.

And in the process, I am becoming more of who I am (iM) every day.

5

Step into Greatness

The iMatter Journey is a lifelong experience of enlightenment and self-mastery. As you practice Think–Act–Be (to keep you in the iMatter mindset) and use the other tools in the iMatter Journey, you will move step-by-step into your greatness with *Commitment*, *Clarity*, and *Confidence*.

These three steps guide you along the path to freedom, joy, and peace. As you move along in your own iMatter Journey, you'll climb out of "Am I?" doubt and uncertainty and reach I am or iM certainty and self-mastery. In short, you'll *be* exponentially YOU.

THE ✳iMATTER JOURNEY™

STEPPING INTO YOUR GREATNESS

COMMITMENT

MINDSET

PROCESS

TOOLS

RITUALS

+

CLARITY

WHY

HOW

WHAT

+

CONFIDENCE

COMMUNITY

CRAFT

RELATIONSHIPS

HEALTH

SPIRIT

=

SELF MASTERY

✳iM

IMATTER.COM

48

Steps of the iMatter Journey

Self-mastery is a big concept that may seem intimidating at first. Here's the good news: You don't arrive at self-mastery in one huge leap. You move toward it slowly. With each step, your clarity sharpens, as does your vision for the future and the confidence to make your unique impact on the world.

Commitment + Clarity + Confidence = Self-mastery (iM)

Self-mastery is about growing, developing, and expanding into your greatness. As you learn to look at the world and your life in new ways and become more introspective and less self-critical, you will elevate your mind. You will become more focused on what matters and less distracted by how others define success.

Your new mindset and focus will enable you to expand your impact simply by being who you are. When you offer your unique skills and abilities to the world, everyone benefits. The more you live out who you are and pursue what matters to you, the more confident you become because you see the value of your impact on those around you.

In Parts 3, 4, and 5, we'll explore this deeper as well as dive into Lifetime Expanders. These fundamental principles are like mile markers along your path. They inspire you to elevate your mind, expand your impact, and ultimately know and act like *you* matter!

LIFETIME
EXPANDERS™

There are seven key lifetime expanders:

1. CREATE GREAT RELATIONSHIPS
2. CHOOSE YOUR ATTITUDE
3. REALIZE WHAT MATTERS MOST
4. CLARIFY WHO YOU ARE
5. FOLLOW YOUR NORTH STAR
6. LIVE YOUR LEGACY, NOW
7. BE, REGARDLESS

Are you ready to take the first step?

PART 3

Commitment

The first step of the iMatter Journey is to commit to *yourself* and the belief that *you matter*. I invite you to practice saying it right now—iMatter!

Trust the process. Remember, this isn't a sprint or a 5K. It's not even a marathon. This journey is more like an ultra-triathlon. To stay on track, you must commit to using the process, the tools, the rituals, and most importantly, to the iMatter mindset that will see you through to the very end.

COMMITMENT

MINDSET   PROCESS

TOOLS   RITUALS

6

Elevate Your Mind

This is so much more than a self-help book—this book is about empowering *you* to *help yourself* by making time to elevate your mind and tap into your inner wisdom.

To get the most out of the iMatter Journey, you will need to override common, limiting beliefs and reset your mental space by changing your default settings regarding the way you *view* and *do* life. These beliefs impact your relationships, mental strength, confidence, attitude, and your results. If you've practiced Think-Act-Be, you've already started that mental decluttering. Great job!

In this step—Commitment—we'll continue that process by implementing the first two Lifetime Expanders: Create Great Relationships and Choose Your Attitude.

Lifetime Expander 1—Create Great Relationships

The first Lifetime Expander is to Create Great Relationships because it will impact your every encounter.

Throughout my journey, I have found that creating great relationships is key to having a fulfilling, peaceful, happy time during my stay on Planet Earth. Positive connections with others provide ample opportunity to learn more about myself, elevate my mind, feel more deeply, and grow as both the human and spiritual being I truly am.

This is why great relationships are essential. They expand our capacity for growth and wisdom.

What is the greatest relationship in your life? Is it with your spouse? Your kids? Your parents? Your business partners?

Ultimately, I've come to realize that, while all those people are valuable and important, it's actually the relationship with *myself* that is most critical—iMatter most. Yes, that's right; in my world, iMatter most. It's important to "love thyself" first if you're going to be able to give love to *anyone* else.

My selfishness is selfless. Think of what flight attendants say about oxygen masks in the preflight safety presentation: "Be sure to adjust your own mask before helping others." I believe that's also true for life outside the plane: If you adjust yourself before helping others, you can ultimately be of greater service.

So first, practice self-love by attending to your needs.

For many people, practicing self-love seems much harder than loving others. Rather than truly caring for themselves, they find all kinds of ways to fill the void created by self-neglect, or worse, self-loathing. Some overeat, buy stuff they don't need, shame themselves and others, and blame and deprive themselves of connection. Why? Often fear of rejection or feeling unworthy is the root cause. We can only experience love and feel connected with others as much as we love ourselves and feel connected to our own spirit, and that is true for all.

One of the most powerful things I have learned from loving myself is the importance of being vulnerable—with others and with myself. Brené Brown, author of *Daring Greatly* and an expert on vulnerability, says, "Vulnerability is about showing up and being seen. It's tough to do that when we're terrified about what people might see or think."

Unfortunately, most of us are so scared of being vulnerable enough to acknowledge and share our true selves that we resort to meaningless or harmful pursuits. We don't make time for ourselves. We treat ourselves more harshly than we would ever treat another soul.

In the iMatter Journey, the Create Great Relationships Lifetime Expander uses our connection with others as practice for relating and connecting to ourselves. As I observe how I relate to others, the respect and compassion I have for them, I learn to be more gentle with myself. In short, I practice treating myself with the same kindness, affection, respect, and compassion I often more easily extend to others. Having spent years developing this practice, I've also found that, when I get into fiery situations with someone close to me, I can respond with more integrity, compassionate honesty, and kindness in the moment because I have established a deeper, more authentic relationship with myself.

Being vulnerable—the key to building a great relationship—takes great courage, faith, and trust, which means we need to set some ground rules. The iMatter Rules of Engagement™ is a tool that helps us open our hearts for deeper connection. This iMatter tool is one you'll return to on a daily basis.

iMatter Tool: The iMatter Rules of Engagement

Great relationships don't just happen. It's tough to connect and go deep with someone without respect and trust. That's where the Rules of Engagement tool comes into play. You can establish this simple set of ground rules with any person or group with whom you want to develop a deeper relationship. When everyone agrees to abide by these rules, it opens the door to greater trust and more meaningful connections.

THE IMATTER RULES OF ENGAGEMENT™

CREATE A SAFE SPACE	ESTABLISH BOUNDARIES	IMPLEMENT STRUCTURE
BE AWARE OF VERBIAGE *eliminate exaggerations, the words better and should*	OK TO ASK FOR HELP	MEETING RHYTHMS *set a time and be consistent*
SPEAK FROM THE "I": SPEAK FROM EXPERIENCE	OK TO ASK FOR WHAT I WANT	USE TOOLS
LISTEN TO UNDERSTAND - NOT RESPOND	OK TO REMIND ME (PERMISSION)	KEEP IT CONFIDENTIAL

CREATE A SAFE SPACE

Create a safe space where every participant in the conversation can speak openly and honestly without fear of judgment, ridicule, or criticism. The following will help to create a safe space:

1. Be aware of verbiage—eliminate exaggerations and the words *better* and *should*.

Exaggerations, by definition, are never true, yet they are often thrown about in heated conversations. The same is true for words like *better* ("It would be better if you did it this way.") and *should* ("You should not do that.") that can come across as critical or judgmental.

Creating a safe space begins with an awareness of the words we use, regardless of whether we are speaking to others or ourselves. Verbiage often reflects consciousness. If your words are harsh, the recipient will believe it reflects your feelings toward them.

2. Speak from the "I"; speak from experience.

As discussed in Chapter 1, wisdom and learning can come through dialogue. A way to share wisdom is by sharing and speaking from the I. In other words, share your experiences. Telling someone what to do often turns them off or shuts them down. But when you speak from experience ("I know what you mean. I've felt the same way. When I was in a similar situation, what helped me was . . ."), it's easy to connect on common ground and share wisdom in a non-threatening, non-commanding way. As a result, the listener often remains more open to the conversation.

3. Listen to understand, not to respond.

Interrupting, even if you *think* you know where the person's train of thought is going, shows a lack of respect for the other person. It chips away at the walls of your safe space.

Listening to understand (without interrupting) means letting the other person finish speaking and only then, asking clarifying questions.

Establish Boundaries

Establishing permissions or boundaries in your relationships sets the stage for open and honest communication. And that's where the magic happens.

With the goal of creating connection through great relationships, here are the three boundaries or permissions to use within trusted relationships:

1. It's okay to ask for help.

Asking for help *doesn't* make you a burden. It honors the other person's gifts and shows your vulnerability and trust in that person—all of which lead to deeper relationships.

If I have people around me who are more competent than me in a particular area, why *wouldn't* I ask them for a helping hand? And if my unique talents can be of service to a friend or colleague, I certainly want them to ask me for help. There is no need to get stuck on a problem when you know the person next to you may have a solution. It's okay to ask for help but make sure you allow space for the person to say no.

2. It's okay to ask for what I want.

When being open and honest in relationships (both personal and professional), it's okay to share our preferences, goals, and dreams. Too often, people beat around the bush when it comes to what they want, from the simple to the seemingly impossible. Want to take that vacation? Share it with your professional team to see if they can help get you there. Been dying to see the latest movie? Tell your partner! Do you want that hard-to-get speaker for your next event? Ask.

Too often, people focus solely on pleasing others and not taking care of themselves. But this is the iMatter Journey we're installing, and you are affirming that *you matter*. Your needs and desires matter. Sure, the person can always say no, but if you don't ask, you aren't giving them an opportunity to say yes and strengthen that relationship.

3. It's okay to remind me.

As we set and share goals with our teams, it is beneficial, also, to give people permission to touch base and check on our progress. Tell your team or others you trust that it's okay to remind you of your goals and who you've said you want to be.

If I have given my team permission to call me out when I'm off track, I know they're coming from a place of concern and sincerity.

But if I call someone out who hasn't granted me permission to do so, well, that may come off as just plain rude. The person may go into defensive mode and put up a wall of, "I don't have to answer to you!"

IMPLEMENT STRUCTURE

As a Visionary, if I am left to myself, I run from structure. I love the spontaneity of tapping into magic and flow. I have realized, however, that when I put structure around things that matter most, such as my business, my family, my health, and my relationships, I am creating room for magic and spontaneity within that structure.

We use the rhythms, tools, and confidentiality to implement structure in our lives.

1. Create rhythms.

If I'm trying to create a great relationship, but I don't spend time regularly with my leadership team, wife, or kids, I'm probably not going to go to the next level with those relationships. Rhythms can be implemented by fanatically scheduling the time to meet and do a check-in with your team. Have a weekly date with your spouse and kids. Consider scheduling time daily, weekly, quarterly, and annually to discuss your collective and individual goals. Set up a calendar reminder, so you don't forget, and try not to constantly reschedule. I've found that I experience fewer communication issues when my meeting rhythms are in place.

2. Use and commit to tools.

Find systems, structures, or tools that work for your business, life, and key relationships (business partner, spouse, kids). It can be as simple as using the same calendar or planning platforms (Google, Apple, Trello, Basecamp, etc.) or as using the iMatter tools for yourself and your team. When you and the people around you share common tools and vocabulary, it helps you all be more successful.

3. Keep it confidential.

Relationships grow and deepen when we are open and honest and share our true feelings. Trust is essential to that growth and sharing. Breaking confidentiality breaks trust. To ensure you're in a safe space, ask for confidentiality before divulging something private. Honor the relationship by keeping what you discuss private.

In addition to the Rules of Engagement, we've developed two other tools that equip us to Create Great Relationships. The Take 5 Check-In™ and the daily 3-3-1™ tools help you look inward and connect with yourself. Remember, that's where great relationships begin.

"Act the way you want to be and soon you'll be the way you act."

–Les Brown

iMatter Tool: The Take 5 Check-In

The Take 5 Check-In is the cornerstone tool in the iMatter Journey and is about tapping into your head and heart to find the answers within. This quick weekly exercise gives you a structure for gaining clarity about what's going on in and around you and reinforcing values and goals. When you Take 5, you make time in your busy, distracted life to learn about and mentor yourself. It is something you can do alone and then, if you choose to, share with a valued friend, spouse, teammate, or team to create more intimate connections and inspire open dialogue.

Why Use the Take 5 Check-In?

The Take 5 Check-In creates the opportunity to get your frustrations, your big questions, and the distracting chatter or thoughts that plague you out of your head and onto paper. (You can also use your phone, a whiteboard, or a computer.) It doesn't matter whether your frustrations or fears are life-threatening, minor, or somewhere in between. They take up valuable mental space, and their constant noise stunt your creativity. Once those inhibitors are out of your head, you'll start to feel a quieting and freeing elevation of your mind. Without those distractions, you move into your week and your life with more courage and confidence, ready to tackle what lies ahead.

The key component to the Take 5 Check-In is getting distracting or discouraging thoughts out of the swirling trap of your mind—unscattering the chatter—and creating a safe space to acknowledge them. Then you can let go of ones that are not serving you and choose your next step. Sharing your Take 5 in a safe space with people you trust allows for dialogue and shared wisdom and creates greater trust and connection in your relationship.

As I do my Take 5 Check-In, I hear patterns, thoughts, keywords, and, most importantly, any topics or issues to tackle—to-dos or things I want to get done or things that I can ask for help with or delegate to others. I may hear a potential blog, podcast, or other creative ideas. Often, when I am sharing my Take 5 with the people on my team, they can capture those ideas and action items and get to work implementing them.

As I get things out of my head, I'm more apt to flip the negativity to positivity, put things in perspective, and feel more at peace and less stressed. Greater positivity, peace, and freedom allow me to be present in the moment. I can focus on the people I am with and expand my impact on their lives and my own. This clarity and positivity also enable me to be open to the synchronicities and the magic that unfold around me each day; I can see and take advantage of opportunities I might not notice if I remained limited or distracted by fears and frustrations. Ultimately, the Take 5 takes me from the urgent to the important as I elevate my mind and get into the flow, solve larger issues, or focus on next steps and opportunities.

When done regularly, the Take 5 Check-In can help you unscatter the chatter of how you *think* so you can *act* and *be* differently in your life. This sets the stage for more productivity, fulfillment, happiness, faith, courage, and connection. *Note*: I suggest using this tool weekly—make time each week to focus on *you*! Remember, as you change your thinking, you change your life.

BOB SHENEFELT

THE TAKE 5 CHECK-IN™   **iMATTER**

FRUSTRATIONS

FRUSTRATION	WHY	NEXT STEPS

DREADS

DREAD	WHY	NEXT STEPS

AM I?

Ah-ha

WHAT	WHY	NEXT STEPS

UNSCATTER THE CHATTER

CELEBRATIONS

CELEBRATION	WHY	NEXT STEPS

OPPORTUNITIES

OPPORTUNITY	WHY	NEXT STEPS

GRATITUDE

THING	WHY	NEXT STEPS

I AM ...

How to Use the Take 5 Check-In (Practice Weekly)

To get the most from this tool, you'll want to fanatically schedule about thirty minutes of uninterrupted time for it once a week. Find a comfortable spot (for me, it's *not* my home) and have a yellow legal pad, iPad or reMarkable, whiteboard, or whatever you can record things on to get it out of your head so you can make space for clarity and creativity. When you read or share your Take 5 aloud, it will take about five minutes, which is where the tool gets its name.

Begin by acknowledging the negative. Reality is reality. The things you don't want won't go away if you ignore them; in fact, left unchecked, negative thoughts tend to grow. You can stop that growth by recognizing what it is, why it bothers you, and then either letting it go or planning for what you're going to do about it.

1. Frustrations

Frustrations are the obstacles in your path. They may be self-imposed or intentionally or unintentionally placed there by others.

- **WHAT:** Ask yourself, "Is there something in the way of my happiness or progress that is frustrating me?" List your top frustrations in the "What" column. Express it. Be honest with yourself and don't overthink it—you may not have three every time!
- **WHY:** Now, take a few moments to reflect on *why* you're frustrated about those things. Ask yourself, "What is the emotion behind this frustration? What is the root or cause?" In the "Why" column, list your answers next to the respective frustration.

- **NEXT STEPS:** In the third column, list what Next Steps you can take in response to the What and Why to shift or resolve the frustration. These are actions you will want to prioritize this week. It could be to do the Flip It™ exercise on page 93 of this book.

2. Dreads

Dreads are anything you're not looking forward to. By expressing them during a check-in, you have a chance to own up to your emotions and then view them as issues you need to deal with. Using the same process you did for frustrations, take a few moments to contemplate the following:

- **WHAT:** What are you not looking forward to? What would you rather put off, or what have you been putting off?
- **WHY:** Why are you dreading these things?
- **NEXT STEPS:** This may not be the end-all solution, but list the next step(s) you can take to shift, minimize, or eliminate the dreads.

3. "Am I?"

In the same way you voice your frustrations and dreads, take time to voice your doubts about yourself. The conversation in most people's heads is often negative. My biggest bully is me to myself. Maybe you can relate. Before we can shift the conversation, it helps to become aware of internal **My biggest bully is me to myself.** dialogue undermining our confidence. Get it out into the daylight so you can expose untruths. More on how to shift the conversation later in this chapter.

4. *Ah-ha*

An *ah-ha* can be a realization of a truth that you may have overlooked. It could also be the solution you've been looking for that all of a sudden becomes clear as you process your thoughts verbally.

- **WHAT:** List the realizations you have had since your last Take 5 Check-In in the "What" column.
- **WHY:** What is the root of each *ah-ha*?
- **NEXT STEPS:** If the *ah-ha* or realization calls for a change, note it in the "Next Steps" column.

Often when people start this, they do not have any *ah-ha* moments. Go back through the earlier steps and review your responses. You may notice that you have repeated an issue, for instance. Your *ah-ha* might be as simple as recognizing that you have a choice to decide to do something about it.

5. Celebrations

We generally don't take time to celebrate something unless it feels big. When you are doing your Take 5, give yourself some credit. Find those things that deserve to be noticed and celebrated. Many times, after I record my Take 5, I think, *Wow! I really had a great week! Look at all the things to celebrate!* It could be something a family member did, a business success, an exercise routine; it can be big or small. Take a moment to acknowledge what's worth honoring and then incorporate celebrating into a next step. If something went great, why not do it again?

- **WHAT:** What's great about life right now? This could be anything from time with family at my son's baseball game to hiring a new team member. Celebrate anything that brings joy, then list those celebrations in the "What" column.

- **WHY:** Explain why each celebration brings you joy in the "Why" column.
- **NEXT STEPS:** List some next steps to help you enjoy this experience even more deeply or manifest more happiness in your life.

6. Opportunities

Opportunities pop up all the time. Unless we catalog and share those opportunities, they might not find a way onto our to-do lists and into our lives. Including opportunities in the Take 5 Check-In influences our daily priorities by keeping our minds open to possibilities.

- **WHAT:** What opportunities are currently in front of you? Consider every aspect of life, not just work.
- **WHY:** Explain why it's an opportunity now.
- **NEXT STEPS:** List some next steps to help you focus on each opportunity so you can get the most out of them.

7. Gratitude

Putting positive energy out into the universe elicits positive energy in return. It's the logic of the Be–Do–Have mindset that we are tapping into through Think-Act-Be. By being conscious of what you're grateful for and sharing that gratitude, you open your life to even more goodness.

- **WHAT:** Think of the things, people, or relationships you're most thankful for.

- **WHY:** Share why you're grateful for them.
- **NEXT STEPS:** List some next steps to help you take action or pay it forward, such as writing a thank-you note to someone.

8. "I Am"

After this exercise, I can often turn many of the "Am I?" questions I've listed into "I Am" affirmations. Again, it's a choice to shift the conversation (more on how to do this later). If I can't merely change the words to achieve a mind-set shift, then I decide if it's something that matters most to me. If so, I make an action item or goal to address it. If not, I let it go.

For this section, you will write a series of statements or affirmations as follows:

- Flip as many "Am I?" doubts into "I Am" statements or affirmations as you can; for example, if you wrote "Am I a good boss?" before, write "I Am a good boss" now.
- List any additional "I Am" statements or affirmations that resonate with you, too. Some that I often write include: I am grateful. I am at peace. I am present in the moment. I am in love.

Take a look at each of the categories. What did you identify as a frustration or a dread? Were you able to further understand why you have the feelings you do around those things? Were you able to develop a realistic next step to alleviate your anxiety around them? This could be as simple as deciding to let it go or flip it.

Did you notice any unexpected *ah-ha* moments or discoveries? How easily did you identify reasons to celebrate, uncover opportunities, and find things to be grateful for? Did the exercise open you up to any new possibilities?

iMatter Tool: Notes to Self™

When reviewing your Take 5 Check-In, look for themes. Use the Notes to Self tool to record these themes as well as your *ah-has* and big ideas, topics for later, get-tos, love-tos, and those have to-dos, or items you either need help with or want to delegate. *Note*: You'll use the Notes to Self tool in conjunction with several other iMatter tools as means to track what is important to you. Keep it handy!

Many next steps come from this exercise, but sometimes addressing a few main themes will immediately knock out a bunch of them. The clarity you find can drive growth and future projects. Either take it upon yourself to get these things done or delegate them to your team. Capturing these to-do items and adding them to your top action items each day (something you'll do when you use the 3-3-1 tool that's coming up next) makes them seem more manageable and less intimidating. See iMatter.com/UnscatterTheChatter for an example of a completed Take 5 Check-In.

Using the Take 5 Check-In over time, I've found I have fewer frustrations and fears and more celebrations and opportunities. I've also noticed that my self-talk has shifted to be more positive. My relationships are richer, and I create and feel more connection. I'm mentoring myself through the process, which has changed my life!

BOB SHENEFELT

GET TO / LOVE TO

HAVE TO / NEED TO / DELEGATE / ASK FOR HELP

TOPICS / TO DISCUSS

AH-HAS / KEYWORDS / THEMES / BIG IDEAS

Practicing the Take 5 Check-In for a Group Setting

To get the most out of this tool, *sharing is key.* In a group set-ting, the magic of the Take 5 Check-In is that you're all in it together. Everyone comes to the table with their completed Take 5 Check-In and follows the process below to share them. If people have not had time to complete it before, allot ten minutes of your meeting to allow people to com-plete their Take 5 Check-In. Then spend five minutes each sharing what you wrote down. There is tremendous value in knowing what is on your team members' minds. Having open dialogue helps everyone learn, grow together, and share wisdom.

Once everyone has shared, you may choose to spend some time discussing the topics and brainstorming action items and solutions. Even if it takes thirty minutes out of a one-hour meeting, you'll benefit from identifying what is weighing on everyone's heads and hearts.

Of course, we start with the aforementioned iMat-ter Rules of Engagement. (See page 56.) For the Take 5, I implement a specific structure to ensure there are no inter-ruptions and that no one person dominates the conversation.

By honoring the guidelines below, participants keep their responses brief, and nothing is discussed in detail until everyone's thoughts are on the table.

1. Keep an eye on the time and consider setting a five-minute timer for each person's sharing to keep your check-in session on track.
2. Decide which person will be the first to share. Then they can begin to review the answers they listed in each section, not to exceed five minutes.

3. When listening to someone else's Take 5 Check-In, capture any clarifying questions and potential topics on your Notes to Self page but hold your questions until everyone has shared.
4. Once everyone has shared their Take 5 Check-In, go back to the first person who shared and build a list of questions and topics for discussion. If a question requires more than a short answer, keep it on the list for an extended discussion.
5. Go through this process for each participant. Use the remaining time to prioritize the items on the list and discuss them.

The Take 5 moves the urgent out of my head so I can elevate my mind and tune into what's important and get into the flow of *being*. When shared with my team and my spouse or partner, we know what is going on with one another and can look for ways to share the load or delegate.

The iMatter tools, like the Take 5 Check-In and the 3-3-1 which follows, give me a clear mind, so I can make connections, create great relationships, conquer negativity, and focus on what matters most.

iMatter Tool: The 3-3-1

I developed the 3-3-1 tool to honor myself by remembering what matters most and keeping my focus strong and clearly defined. It's a daily ritual as much as it is a tool, and I make time for it at least five days each week. The 3-3-1 is my morning meditation to tap into my inner wisdom and start my day with peace and clarity. It is amazing how committing just a few minutes to myself can shift my whole day *and my life*.

Each morning, I ask myself three questions. The answers provide direction, clarity, and purpose and give me permission to own my day, my quarter, and my life. No matter what comes up, if I accomplish the three things that matter most and my top three to-do or action items, I am golden.

I may choose to continue working and get more done, or I may choose to hang out with my family. I can help others more authentically and without the feeling of something hanging over my head. No matter what I do with the rest of my day, I still have a sense of accomplishment knowing that I've moved forward on something important to me.

THE 3-3-1 ™   **iMATTER**

WHAT MATTERS MOST

1. _____
2. _____
3. _____

TOP 3 ACTION ITEMS

1. _____
2. _____
3. _____

IF IT WERE UP TO ME

1. _____

RULES OF ENGAGEMENT

CREATE A SAFE PLACE	ESTABLISH BOUNDARIES	IMPLEMENT STRUCTURE
Be aware of verbiage	Okay to ask for help	Meeting rhythms—set a time and be consistent
Speak from the "I." Speak from experience	Okay to ask for what I want	Use tools
Listen to understand—not to respond	Okay to remind me—permission	Keep it confidential

How to Use the 3-3-1

I love how quick, simple, and powerful this exercise is. It literally takes just a few minutes a day. It allows me to feel more connected and my team to stay focused and in sync with one another. I take a couple of minutes in a quiet environment—it could be my office, hot tub, or front porch—to check in and ask myself three questions.

1. What Matters Most (3)

Since this is a daily ritual, the question *What matters most?* is about the three things that matter most to me *today*. *Note*: These are not *urgent* things; they're *important* things. This tool keeps my eyes on the prize and prevents me from getting caught up in the mundane. What matters most could be driving revenue, nurturing key relationships, or focusing on my health or my family. By writing them down, I am committing to focusing my energy on what matters most to me *today*.

2. Top Three Action Items (3)

Next, I address my top three action items. If I get these three things done, it will be a great day. These may have some urgency and they are also important. These items are above and beyond my normal "day job" and must be specific and quantifiable so it is clear when they are complete. By deciding what is most important today, this present moment, I can Imagine a great future, Improve on the past, and Impact the moment. I know that *this* moment is where I can have the greatest impact. See page 91 for more about how to use this formula to Flip It.

3. If It Were Up to Me (1)

Lastly, the "If It Were Up to Me" section acknowledges that sometimes I *think* things are out of my hands. It then shifts the conversation, emphasizing something good or realizing that I do have some control in the situation. In fact, I may realize it *is* up to me. This practice puts me into a state of gratitude and shifts my focus to an affirmation which sets my intention for the day. For example, I may start with "I hope today is great," and then I shift that conversation into "Today is great." I am setting that intention that if it were up to me (And actually, it is!), I am going to have amazing breakthroughs today.

Example of the 3-3-1

It's simple to start by doing a quick-and-dirty jot like this example:

What Matters Most
- Courage
- Discipline
- My wife and I are on the same page

Top Three Impact Items
- Three calls to target market prospects
- Review PowerPoint for my speech
- Send 5 notes of gratitude

If It Were Up to Me
- If it were up to me, today is awesome

Other examples I have used in the past are: I am love, I am being, I love being alive, I am honored to serve, I am prepared, I am wide awake, I am experiencing life today, I am smiling, I am breathing deeply. Sometimes I use the same one two days in a row. It's whatever is affirming to *you*! It is up to *you*!

Take a few minutes to complete the 3-3-1. Then spend some time to reflect on what the tool is showing you and how your conversation is shifting.

Why Do the 3-3-1?

The 3-3-1 gives you time to think and helps with focus, choosing a positive attitude, and being motivated to make each day a great day and knock out your top action items right away. I have gained confidence that I can get more of the important things done, go have lunch with my wife—or do whatever it is I want to do—because I have already had a successful day. If I have forty things that I need to get done today and get twenty completed, I can become frustrated at the twenty things I did not get done. If these are the top three most important—not just urgent—I am building a habit to have focus and knock out those things that make the greatest impact.

When I make time to do the daily check-in and then share my 3-3-1, there is much more accountability, and it helps me stay in the flow as I make the time because iMatter enough to spend a few minutes each morning. We encourage people to create 3-3-1 teams with which to share their 3-3-1s and support one another. Teams may include your spouses, coworkers, clients, etc. I find that if I write down my 3-3-1 and share it, I am much more apt to get it done. Also, when I ask someone to be on my team, all I ask is that they glance at my 3-3-1 to support me. I often find that I get responses from people that say, "Hey, good luck with that" or "How did this go?"

One day, I had a health goal, and my action item was to find a foot doctor. Three people responded with foot doctors in the area. My mom is on my 3-3-1 team, and she checked in to ask how I felt because she noticed on my 3-3-1 that I mentioned a doctor's appointment. At a glance, I am sharing my vulnerability with people that matter most to build great relationships. They support me as I support them when we share our 3-3-1s and we feel more connected not only to each other but to ourselves.

Making your goals public reinforces your commitment to completing them. In addition, you can lean on those you've shared your goals with for help and support.

> "Bob shared his 3-3-1 tool one morning during our regular coffee get-together, and I could have never imagined how transformative it would become in my daily routine. The tool keeps me focused and grounded. I love it so much that my entire executive team and sales team are now using it and sharing it with each other every morning!"
>
> —Rob Dube, Co-CEO and Co-Founder of imageOne and Visionary for The 10 Disciplines with Gino Wickman

When groups or teams share their daily 3-3-1, they gain a greater awareness of what's going on in their teammates' world. You can share your 3-3-1 verbally, in writing, or using your favorite communication app.

Your mindset is critical to your perspective of your world, both inside and outside of you. It helps us put life in perspective, the thoughts we have around the spiritual and the material—the *being* and the *having*.

Combining the Take 5 and 3-3-1 with the tools we will discuss next, you will experience the incredible clarity that comes with intentionality and focus on what you want to energize in your life and let go of what is no longer serving you and is holding you back.

"Every worthy goal written down and shared is bound to happen."

—Earl Nightingale

7

It's Your Choice

Living out your commitment to yourself that *you mat-ter* requires intentionality. The Choose Your Attitude Lifetime Expander reminds you that you are not your thoughts or the chatter in your head. You have a choice in how you react to your thoughts, which means you are not at the mercy of the chatter. You can choose to control your attitude, and ultimately, your life.

Lifetime Expander 2—Choose Your Attitude

Central to iMatter is the concept that how I *think* changes the way I experience the world. If I'm obsessed with what's going wrong, I will be miserable. I came up with a mantra: *It Starts with Me—It's Not All About Me.* This is a reminder that I have choices about how I face the challenges and obstacles of my day. As Don Miguel Ruiz says in *The Four Agreements*, don't take things personally. Bad things aren't happening to me because something or someone is out to get me. I couldn't control that even if they were. I can choose to take action around what I can control, which is my attitude.

Attitude is everything.

Attitude is, in fact, an intentional choice, so *choose your 'tude!* It's easy to get caught up in disappointments and frustrations, but disappointments and frustrations are part of life. I can't change that any more than you can. What we can change is the way we respond. We can also choose to do the things and *think* about the things that will increase our happiness no matter what is going on around us.

In *Bridge of Spies*, Tom Hanks's character is a lawyer representing a spy about to go to trial. The spy seems surprisingly calm about the dire situation. In the course of their conversations, Hanks's character asks, "Do you never worry?" To which the spy responds, "Well, does it help?"

That simple question provoked a paradigm shift for me. The spy knew that worry would not help him in any way. It wouldn't empower him or change the outcome. I realized the same is true for me. Worry offers no benefit. To the contrary, it drains me, and if I let it, worry can ruin my whole day. Why would I spend my time and mental and emotional energy on something so destructive?

The fear of the future and the regret of the past can hold me back if I allow them to, or they can be a learning opportunity. I choose, therefore, to shift my perception of worries, fears, and frustrations. I don't deny that things aren't perfect. I simply *choose* to focus on what I want to expand in my life (imagine a great future) and on letting go and being grateful despite my circumstances (improve on the past). When my

84

focus is calm and unworried, I can show up and be present in the now (impact the moment). There's that formula again: Imagine, Improve, Impact.

"What you imagine, you create."
—Buddha

iMatter Tool: Shift the Conversation

Our inner voice chatters constantly. It is often judgmental about others and ourselves. *Am I this, or am I that? Am I good enough? Am I a good father? Will I ever be happy?* This conversation is ongoing, so why not be a part of it and make it uplifting rather than depressing?

The condemning voice does not speak the truth about who you are, so rather than allowing it to dictate the tone and direction of the conversation, take control. Elevate your mind by taking accountability and responsibility for what you are thinking. In other words, shift the conversation.

SHIFT THE CONVERSATION

Often, we believe what the inner voice is saying, so why not have that voice be positive? Be a part of the conversation. Don't let it be a one-way conversation.

Michael Singer explains in *The Untethered Soul: The Journey Beyond Yourself* that the mind is constantly talking. The voice takes both sides of the conversation, and it never shuts up. Many people live their lives through that conversation and miss out on the actual experience.

When you recognize that you are not your thoughts but that you are, instead, an observer of that chatter, you can shift the conversation.

As mentioned in the Rules of Engagement, our verbiage—what we say and what we think—reflects our consciousness. If my mental verbiage is negative or full of doubt and criticism, it is an indication of the state of my mindset, spirit, and soul. On the flip side, speaking positively and calling it forth can positively impact my consciousness. I can choose my attitude by shifting the conversation in my mind. This helps me tap into the Think–Act–Be process. As I *think* differently, I then *act* differently, and ultimately I will *be* differently. The outcome of that Think-Act-Be shift is that I end up *doing* and *having* different outcomes in my relationships and in my life.

How to Use the Shift the Conversation Tool (Practice as Needed)

To shift the conversation in my head and heart, I must first recognize that a conversation is going on in my mind and that I have a part in that conversation. I am not a victim of my inner voice because I have the power to shift the conversation. I can turn that voice in my head into a friend rather than an enemy, and, in making that shift, I have the power to change my attitude, which affects the outcome in life.

How can you shift the conversation?

Sometimes getting the tangle of thoughts and questions out of your head helps to unscatter the chatter and determine what is real or true for you. Identify the doubting "Am I?" questions and turn them into "I am" affirmations. Remember, we tend to believe what we think, so make sure your thoughts are true. When you take control of your thoughts, you change what you believe, which changes how you speak, act, and experience life. That's harnessing the power of iM or self-mastery!

Step 1: Notice "Am I" Questions

Take a minute and write down some of your doubts or beliefs about yourself in the form of Am I questions:

AM I _____?
AM I _____?
AM I _____?

Here's an example: If my inner voice asks, "Am I successful?" that doubting question represents a thought based on a belief about myself, that *I'm not successful.*

Step 2: Shift to Affirmations of I Am

Shift the doubting question to an affirming statement—for example, *I am successful.* By repeating that statement and acknowledging my innate value, those new words change how you feel about yourself. Repeat them often enough, and Think-Act-Be will change your reality.

In the simplest terms, the process guides your thinking and moves you from "Am I?" questions to "I Am" affirmations:

- Am I ever going to be rich? → I am abundantly successful, and I have access to everything I need.
- Am I going to be able to go on vacation? → I am living with freedom and can choose my own schedule.
- Am I able to get out of this situation? → I am free to make decisions and act on them.

If I say, "I am free, I am worthy, I am happy," it changes how I think about my life, success, and career. I begin to believe it and then speak and act as if I am successful and happy; this opens me up to opportunities, freedom, and becoming more able to *be* the person I want to be and therefore to *do* the things I want to do and *have* the life I want to have. Moreover, shifting the conversation from future tense to present tense equates to telling the universe the reality I expect and having faith that it has already happened.

Now it's time to write down the shift of your "Am I" questions above in the form of "I Am" affirmations:

I AM _____.
I AM _____.
I AM _____.

These "I Am" statements can ultimately go on your iMpact Planner (Chapter 11), or you can even write them on sticky notes and put them on your mirror. The goal is to keep reaffirming them.

This tool is part of your weekly Take 5 Check-In, but I encourage you to use it anytime thoughts of doubt, fear, or worry circulate in your mind. It doesn't have to take long. Simply recognize the negative chatter when it happens and shift the mental conversation to one that affirms you.

Remember, your words or verbiage reflect your consciousness. You have the power to call forth that reality you want to experience. The universe responds like a giant copy machine. As you share with others, put out positive energy, and believe that life is already great, you become aware of new opportunities. As your awareness grows and you continue to choose to elevate your mind, you are more likely to seize those opportunities and let fears, limits, and misconceptions fall by the wayside. You begin to know and act like you matter and step into your greatness with conviction.

Shift the Conversation in Action

Once, I was in an argument with my daughter, Grace. She was four at the time, and I was losing the argument and my cool. I never thought that I'd be yelling at my kids, but here I was.

Losing an argument to a four-year-old is bad enough, but then my inner voice kicked in: *Am I any good as a father? Maybe I'm not.*

The thought shocked me. One of the main things that matters most in life to me is being a good father, and in that moment, I doubted myself. I stopped and thought, *Wait a minute, I am a great father!* From that place of awareness, I looked at my present circumstances and considered the argument with my daughter. I asked myself, *Is this how a great father behaves?* The answer was, *No, but **I am** a great father, and I can choose my 'tude and change the course of this discussion with my daughter right now.* So, I did.

I took a deep breath, opened my heart space, and calmly asked my little girl, "When does Daddy get mad?"

She responded, "When I don't listen. I'll go brush my teeth."

Sometimes it's just that easy.

Stating the truths aloud such as, "I am a great father" or "I am a great leader," can have a powerful effect on your inner dialogue and mindset, which impacts your reality. Try it!

Another Example of Shift the Conversation in Action

When John came to me for coaching, he was anxious and hyper-focused on his career. He constantly compared himself, his performance, and his success to others. His inner voice criticized his efforts and outcomes: *When are you going to make it? You're not doing enough!* Using the Shift the Conversation tool, John learned to affirm his substantial successes by giving his inner voice a new script: *I have made huge strides in my career. I am at the top of my game.* Elevating his mind with this positive messaging helped him create a new reality where he felt much more comfortable and confident with his colleagues. That confidence played out, and he took his success to the next level.

Another example was with my client Ted. He and I were golfing with two friends on a beautiful day during the middle of the week. We were having a ball and felt like we were cheating life because instead of working, we were having fun, drinking a beer, and hitting the golf ball around.

Midway through the course, Ted hit an amazing shot onto the green. He was all revved up to make a birdie, but it took two putts to get the ball in the hole. And he was suddenly livid.

Recognizing that his disappointment threatened to ruin what had been an excellent day, I helped him shift the conversation by commenting, "Hey, you hit two great shots, parred the hole, and are on the course with great friends!"

The redirection was simple, but it shifted the conversation in his head, and he ended up playing a great round of golf. So rather than the negative verbiage bringing him and the rest of us down, he shifted the conversation to "I am enjoying the day, I've had some great shots, and I keep improving."

How do you respond to frustrating situations? What attitude about life are you choosing? Remember: You have a choice. When negative emotions or thoughts drive the chatter in your mind, choose to employ a tool, like Shift the Conversation, or the tools that follow, to reframe challenges, irritations, fear, and anger. As you let go of baggage, you free your mind from paralyzing doubt, and you will find the bravery to help you move forward on your journey.

iMatter Tool: Flip It

I love the song "Another Day" from the musical *Rent* because it reminds us to move beyond regret and live the life we are meant to have.

Flip It is a powerful formula to help with forgetting regret and turning any anger, fear, or frustration into a learning opportunity. In my life, I've learned that those negative emotions keep coming back, and seem to get bigger, until I have exhibited to myself and the universe that I have learned the necessary lesson. Flip It speeds the learning process because it empowers me to let go of negativity so I can solve the problem and heal my heart. I've found it especially helpful when dealing with persistent hurt from past relationships that threatens current and future relationships.

As with other learning experiences and tools, I follow the formula of Imagine, Improve, Impact. I like to imagine myself climbing a grassy hill. Coming up behind me are my kids and grandkids. Ahead of me are my parents and grandparents. The hurts, anger, and fear they experienced roll down the hill to me. If I don't deal with it, it continues to grow and roll down the hill to my children and grandchildren. I don't want that. I don't want them to deal with even bigger obstacles than I have. I want to improve my relational health so I can positively impact those I love. To do that, I use the Flip It tool. It empowers me to choose my reality, prevent further damage, and energize the life I want.

Flip It helps me maintain the iMatter mindset by acknowledging reality and then reclaiming awareness of my thoughts and actions. It begins with the insight that I don't feel happy or good about myself when there's any anger, fear, or frustration within me. When negative, doubt-filled thoughts take control, I feel unworthy; I don't act like myself or act like iMatter.

When I flip that anger, fear, or frustration, I move through the emotion so I can set myself free. If I don't Flip It, I remain stuck in negative emotions and the ensuing negative chatter. I have even come to welcome anger, fear, and frustration because I see them as learning and growth opportunities. Sure, I can hide my doubts from others, at least for a little while. Eventually, however, that negativity will cause more problems as my self-doubt increases and inhibits my ability to create great relationships.

By pausing and taking time to identify what's going on and then flipping it, I can shake off the negativity's grip and learn from it. From there, I can courageously take the next step into my greatness.

FLIP IT WORKSHEET

¡MATTER

INTRODUCTION

Am I?

What is your main fear, anger, or frustration?

Why is it a fear, anger, or frustration?

IMAGINE

Now imagine a greater future 30 days from now. If everything went right, what would happen?

IMPROVE

What is the emotion/feeling now? Sit with that emotion/feeling.

Which event from the past pops up? (the first thought to enter your mind)

Who were the people involved, including yourself, and what did they do?

Now, it's time to forgive them and yourself. I did everything I could, knowing what I knew then, at that time. Knowing what I know now, what could I have done differently then?

Knowing what I know now, what would I do differently today?

IMPACT

Flip it. Rewrite any negative statements in a positive way, AM I? to I AM. Look for "ah-ha" moments.

How to Practice Flip It (Practice as Needed)

1. Ask Am I? questions.

What is it you are questioning about yourself or your life? For me, in this example, I will be sharing Am I alone? Am I a good father? Am I inclusive?

2. Name the anger, fear, or frustration.

What is the root of the negative feelings? What is the trigger? First, figure out the real *what*. For example, I spent a couple of weeks with my family over the holidays. My kids are younger than their cousins, and I found myself getting involved in arranging things for them—playing cards with their cousins, basketball with their uncle—and when things didn't go the way I planned, I got mad. The kids weren't mad; I was. When the red haze cleared, I could see that the anger I was feeling was *my* problem, not theirs. I had expectations that weren't being met, but the kids were happy enough doing their own thing. They didn't need me to entertain them.

3. Identify why it's anger, fear, or frustration.

Now that I have a pretty good grasp of what is bothering me, I begin to understand *why* it is bothering me. Examining the issue may require some deep introspection. I use questions to explore the cause of my emotions: *Why does that scare me? Why would that action elicit such a strong reaction? Why did it make me feel angry or frustrated?*

Back to my example. With reflection, I understood that I wanted the kids to have fun, I wanted my nieces and nephews to be engaged, and I wanted my kids to feel like they mattered and were connected to our family. I got frustrated because I didn't feel like that was happening.

Now it's time to IMAGINE ...

4. **You are the artist and creator of your life. Imagine a future greater than your past. What does your life look like thirty days from now? If everything went right, worries weren't a hindrance, and you had no regrets, then what would happen? How would you feel?**

I am not worried about myself or my kids feeling included, and instead I trust and have faith in how life is unfolding.

Next in the formula is to IMPROVE ...

5. **Go back to the original feeling, take a deep breath, and notice the emotions and feelings that go along with the *why*. Sit with those emotions and feelings.**

For me, the experience triggered feelings of anger, inadequacy, rejection, and loneliness. I was sad, thinking my kids were in emotional pain. In fact, my frustration came not from what my kids were feeling but from what the experience made *me* feel.

6. **Examine the experience in light of the past.**

Ask questions like, *What does this remind me of? When have I felt this way in the past? Who were the people involved, and what did they do?* Acknowledge the past and the emotions or feelings from those experiences. Then sit with them to expedite the healing.

In this example, I realized that my own childhood experiences were at the root of those emotions. As the youngest of my siblings, I often felt left out at family gatherings. The older kids wanted to do things together—without me. That made me feel as if I was not good enough or important enough for them to want to hang out with, and it often left me feeling very sad.

7. Forgive the past.

When you've identified the true source of the negative feelings, forgive. Forgive those you've blamed—and forgive yourself. Acknowledge that you did the best you could at the time. It's a choice. Choosing to forgive does not mean you have to think what happened was okay, but that you are making the choice not to let the past event control your present or your future.

In our example, I realized I needed to choose to forgive the people my child-self held responsible for my sadness: my parents, my brother and sister, and, ultimately, myself.

The final part of the formula is IMPACT ...

8. Flip It.

Ask: *Knowing what I know now, what could I have done differently then?*

I could have enjoyed being with the adults I was with because I loved their attention. I could also have asked for what I wanted and shared my feelings about the experience I wanted.

9. Move forward.

Ask: *Knowing what I know now, what can I do differently today? How could I impact the moment right now?*

Now, I can heal and create opportunities! I shared my feelings with my kids and taught them what I just realized: Ask for what you want. Even if we don't get what we want, it's up to us to choose how we react and what energy we want to carry forward. For me, I choose to be present and enjoy the people I am with, and I'm leading by example: *It is up to me how I feel.* Attitude really is everything!

10. Am I to I Am.

Rewrite any Am I questions to I Am statements and look for ah-ha moments that come up.

> I am not alone.
> I am a great father.
> I am inclusive.

Go to iMatter.com/UnscatterTheChatter to download the Flip It worksheet and to look at where you can Imagine, Improve, and Impact your life right now. I promise it will be worth the time.

Flip It in Action

My sixteen-year-old son, Nick, is one of my best Flip It mentors. When he was only nine, we found out he would need a palette expander. That night, we were lying in his bed, and to my surprise and chagrin, he was incredibly excited about it.

I remember staring at the ceiling and thinking, *Dude, you've got it all wrong. I had braces when I was young, and it was horrible. You're going to hate it. It will be painful and uncomfortable. How can you be excited about this? I debated when I should break it to him. I wondered, should I tell him now or wait until it's about to happen?*

He turned to me and asked, "Do you know why I am looking forward to it?"

"Why?"

"Because it's something different, and it's cool to have something new!" he replied with confidence.

He had the greatest attitude about it, so I saved my cautions for later.

As it turned out, Nick's great attitude won. He adjusted to his expander without any issues. Four months after he had it in, he explained why it wasn't problematic for him. He shrugged and said, "Because I looked forward to it."

If I go through Flip It in my head, I can see how Nick's attitude makes sense. His first thought was to imagine his future: a new, even smile. When he thought about his expander, he thought about how it would help him. I am glad that I kept my thoughts to myself so I didn't let my fears interfere.

A year later, I was driving him to school, and he was complaining about his tennis practice after school. I said, "You know, Nick, a wise person once told me that if you look forward to something, it is much more apt to turn out even greater than you expected."

"Really?"

"Yes, and do you know who taught me that?"

"Who?"

"You did!"

Sure enough, he went to tennis with a good attitude and had a lot of fun.

Attitude really is everything!

Another Example of Flip It in Action

My wife and I do an annual Bike and Brew Day in downtown Detroit with another couple who are our great friends.

On one of our recent trips, we talked about several frustrating pieces of news in our life regarding our kids and disappointments they experienced as things around them were canceled due to Covid-19. We shared how we had watched them cry and saw the devastation they felt as their circumstances snatched their dreams and future from under them.

All those things combined could have dampened the mood and the opportunity for connection in the present moment. But here's the thing: We were healthy and on a bike trip, the weather was beautiful, we were with great friends, and we had plenty to be grateful for. Because we were all familiar with what it means to choose our attitude and our reality, my friend declared, "I am choosing to sit at the positive table." At that moment, we all had a decision to make.

Yes, we were all dealing with feelings of anger, fear, and frustration. At the same time, none of us wanted to let things outside of ourselves ruin our day. With some of our best friends who could also support us and be in the moment with us, we took a minute while each person at the table answered the question: Are you sitting at the positive table or not?

Recognizing the power of choice, we each agreed to make it a great day, express gratitude, and stop letting the negative dominate. It worked. We came up with some solutions to issues we were facing, we chose our attitudes, and had a great day. The bonus was we brought that positive energy home to our kids and families, helping them also shift how they were feeling about their lives.

Sometimes you have to Flip It and let go and remind yourself that "that was then, this is now," so you can choose how you show up in life and be open to unexpected possibilities. And then there are times when you just need to throw that sh*t in the fire.

Bonus iMatter Tool: Throw That Sh*t in the Fire™

At least three times a year, I take a trip to Boulder, Colorado. This is how my Go to the Mountain™ retreat started. I've been making the trek for more than twenty years, and I love every minute that I devote to reconnecting with myself, gaining clarity, and getting to the core of my soul. I hike, participate in sweat-lodge ceremonies, spend time in nature, get a massage or two, visit old friends, and make new connections with others and, most importantly, with myself.

After realizing how influential this trip was for my soul, I invited a few close friends to join me to go to the mountain. So many of them raved about what they got out of the trip that I eventually designed a mountain retreat for Visionary entrepreneurs and leaders so that more people could enjoy the benefits. To date, hundreds of people have gone to the mountain for this powerful event.

You can learn about my annual mountain retreat at GoToTheMountain.com.

One exercise we do during the retreat is what I call Throw That Sh*t in the Fire! As I walk in nature and dig into my inner dialogue, there may be some people, events, or things that I'm holding onto that prevent me from stepping into my greatness and living a meaningful, spiritually significant life. The goal of this exercise is to let go of the sh*t holding me back.

If you have something that you need to heal from, this experiential exercise is for you!

How to Use Throw That Sh*t in the Fire (Practice as Needed or Annually)

Throw That Sh*t in the Fire is a very simple, almost self-explanatory exercise.

1. First, sit down in front of a fire with a paper and pen and take a few deep breaths. You can use a fireplace, bonfire pit, or even a fireproof bowl (just make sure the form of fire that you're using is safe first). Tap into your inner wisdom and write down any anger, fear, or frustration that comes to mind. It can be a person, thing, or activity. Anything you're holding onto and is preventing you from not showing up fully as yourself is fair game. I often think of things I became aware of in the Flip It exercise and include the things I want to forgive or let go of so I can move forward.

2. Next, share this anger, fear, or frustration with your team (family, friends, colleagues, etc.)—or not; maybe it's just you, and that's okay too. At the mountain, we create a safe space to share and listen as each of us shares these blockages and baggage. Sometimes getting an outside perspective of a perceived anger, fear, or frustration allows us to realize that we are not alone. We find wisdom as we share and learn from how others have handled similar situations.

3. Finally, the fun part: Throw That Sh*t—your anger, fear, or frustration (i.e., the paper you wrote it on)— into the fire and watch it burn. *Feel* it dissipate! Pretty soon, it's completely gone. The experience in the moment creates a cathartic, beautiful, and freeing feeling. As you throw it, you can also say something like, "This doesn't serve me. I am letting this go, and I am stepping into my greatness."

After returning home from my most recent retreat, I thought, *Ugh, I should have thrown [that] into the fire while I had the chance*! That's when I realized I don't need to be on the mountain to Throw That Sh*t in the Fire; I can be on a beach, in a hotel downtown, or getting a cup of coffee in the morning. Wherever I am, I can still stop and think about an issue, sit with that feeling, and throw it into a mental fire in my head. It allows me to forgive that person, thing, or activity quickly and, as a result, heal myself.

By introducing this exercise to my clients, family, and friends and encouraging them to Throw That Sh*t in the Fire, I pass on the gift of healing and forgiveness.

Commit to *You*

Elevating your mind begins with making a commitment to believing and acting like you matter. Prioritizing yourself, caring for your mental and emotional well-being, and being mindful of your thoughts and attitudes puts you in a space of freedom where you have the capacity for more love, more joy, and more meaning in your life.

You'll use the tools mentioned in the past two chapters frequently in this iMatter Journey. If you are holding old beliefs, limiting mindsets, or emotional baggage that is keeping you from stepping into your greatness, you may even use them daily. I encourage you to earmark the tools pages for easy reference or access and download fillable templates at iMatter.com/UnscatterTheChatter.

Before we move to the next chapter, take a moment to think about your attitude and your inner dialogue. Remember, verbiage reflects consciousness. Which tool will you use to push yourself toward becoming boldly and unapologetically who you are?

Words have power. Patterns have power. Process has power. Combine the three, and you've got magic. Why not harness that magic and use it to unleash your true self? Begin to orient your thoughts around these Lifetime Expanders—Creating Great Relationships and Choosing Your Attitude—to shift your thinking and elevate your mind. Rely on the tools we've explored as you continue to install the iMatter Journey.

You'll see amazing changes in your life right away.

PART 4

Clarity

A life worth living—a *great* and *meaningful* life—means creating a spiritually significant life. Clarity, the second step of installing the iMatter Journey, helps you find your path to that significance.

The next few chapters focus on the Lifetime Expanders of Realize What Matters Most, Clarify Who You Are, and Follow Your North Star. These three Lifetime Expanders are core principles of the iMatter Journey. They will equip you to take the next step: Clarity. By defining what a meaningful life looks like *to you* and identifying how you can make the greatest impact and why making that impact is important to you, you will start living the legacy you want to leave.

The iMatter Legacy Lens™ is simply your what, how, and why.

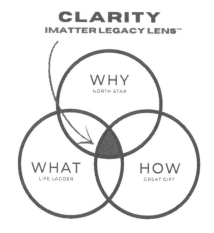

CLARITY
IMATTER LEGACY LENS™

WHY
NORTH STAR

WHAT
LIFE LADDER

HOW
GREAT GIFT

8

Expand Your iMpact

You've committed to the iMatter mindset—to prioritizing yourself and taking responsibility for what you think and say to yourself. My hope is that you feel stronger, more alive, and lighter having released any beliefs or baggage that weighed you down in the past. With a strong foundation, we're taking the next step into clarity. Using the iMatter Legacy Lens, we'll sharpen your focus on your desires and dreams so you can see what matters most—*to you*.

The clarity you will gain in this process will help identify what matters most *right now* because, let's face it, you can't focus on everything at once. Let's get started with the Lifetime Expander: Realize What Matters Most.

Want to Take a Deeper Dive?

The following three chapters provide a high-level overview of how to use your iMatter Legacy Lens: your what (Life Ladder), how (Great Gift), and why (North Star). If you want to dive deep into your soul, we invite you to access the online program we've created to guide you through the iMatter Journey.

Gain clarity around the legacy you want to live and your vision for your life by joining others in the iMatter community. Access this self-guided online journey to help you step into your greatness at TheiMatterJourney.com..

Lifetime Expander 3—Realize What Matters Most

 Figuring out what matters most is like taking a deep dive into your soul. You explore by asking questions like the following:

- What is it that really lights a fire in my spirit and nourishes my soul?
- What inspires me to live with passion and excitement each day?

At first, asking these kinds of questions may feel like wandering into uncharted territory. Our society places little value on listening to the soul's desires. With a focus on academics, testing, and measurable skills, the care of the soul has fallen to the wayside—and with it, our passion, dreams, and drive for joy. How can we feel joyful when we are buried under the pressure of other people's ideas and expectations, worried about the future or regretting the past?

This burying of the soul starts early: Society asks sixth graders to decide what they want to be when they grow up. Schools start putting children as young as eleven years old on trajectories to become doctors, lawyers, or something else deemed equally impressive. By the age of thirty, young doctors, lawyers, and leaders often feel burned out and are left wondering why they have all the *things* and maybe even some of the accolades but are lacking true joy and fulfillment.

Don't worry if you're not used to using words like *spirit* or *soul*. Many people aren't—we're not taught to, after all. But I invite you to start using these words because they have power. My close friend, for example, had been very successful as an entrepreneur. When he discovered iMatter, he got excited precisely by the language of *soul* and *spirit*. He realized his own soul was what he had been missing in his life and professional mindset. Uncovering his soul—and along with it his passion—has changed how he connects with other people and himself.

Maybe you can relate. Maybe you have been going along, head down, focused, working hard, but feeling like *something* is missing. If so, it could be that you have been living someone else's version of success. It happens.

Here's what nobody told me: Unless I'm confident about what I believe, what I want to do, where I want to be, who I want to be with, and how I want others to remember me, someone or something else will decide for me. In fact, they did.

I grew up in a safe, middle-class home in the suburbs of Detroit, with two loving parents and an older brother and sister. To me, it seemed like we didn't have any serious conflicts or challenges, and we certainly didn't discuss any. I didn't struggle with emotions or worry about making something of myself. Life was good, and the expectations were clear and simple: Do your best, be kind, get good grades, go to college, get a job.

Based on the so-called wisdom of a high school aptitude test, I studied business at Western Michigan University. After graduation, I held a couple of different sales jobs, enjoyed partying with my friends, made decent money, and met a girl who seemed to fit into the picture I had in my head at the time. Everyone was settling down, so she and I settled down too. Looking at myself from the outside-in, I seemed to be building the kind of life anyone would hope for. What I didn't appreciate was that it was somebody else's idea of a great life.

I've already told you that I dismantled the prefabricated shell of success after a couple of decades living a life that just wasn't mine. In that cabin by the lake, I knew it wasn't that I had lost myself—the truth was, I had never *found* myself in the first place. I just went along with the crowd and lived up to other people's expectations and worked to meet society's version of success. Sound familiar?

But no more.

With the realization that *I matter*, I developed iMatter. In that process, I also realized that my heart and soul were desperate to be heard and make a difference and leave a mark on this world. For me, sales was *not* the way to do that, nor would I be satisfied just taking another job.

Joseph Campbell was a brilliant mythologist best known for the 1985 television series, *The Power of Myth*. Campbell used to ask people, "Do you know what depression is?" Then he would tell them, "It's when you have spent your life climbing the corporate . . . ladder, and you finally reach the top, and it's against the wrong wall."

I didn't want to keep climbing the same ladder leaning against a wall I didn't like, much less choose. I knew doing so would only lead to more disappointment. With the iMatter mindset that the spiritual and the material need to work in harmony, I adopted and adapted Campbell's Life Ladder analogy. I've since used it to move continually toward the kind of life I want by tapping into the wisdom within, listening to my soul, and choosing the legacy I want to live and leave.

When I began my own iMatter Journey, I didn't know exactly what I wanted to be or do. I realized that I might have to explore a few options to find the right opportunities for me. I developed the My Life Ladder™ tool for myself and my clients so we could grow stronger and more confident as we explored opportunities and relationships or, using the Campbell analogy, walls.

The My Life Ladder tool is incredibly useful in the quest to pursue what matters most to you because it acts as an energy filter for your life. As you use this tool to decide which walls to lean your ladder against, you will create a legacy by living the life you choose.

iMatter Tool: My Life Ladder

Imagine a ladder with five rungs. Each rung stands for a core area of personal well-being: spirit, health, relationships, craft, and community. We use this ladder like an energy filter to explore opportunities and relationships, represented in Campbell's analogy by walls.

MY LIFE LADDER™

The rungs of the Life Ladder build on and connect with each other. If you have an issue with one rung, it affects the other rungs. Each time you climb the ladder, you strengthen the rungs and develop more conviction that they will support you.

Sometimes it's necessary to work on a particular rung. Often you'll spend more time on one than another. You must take the time to listen to your soul to know where on the Life Ladder to focus your time and energy. It's not an algorithm; it's a map of your internal kingdom. (Before continuing, you may want to take a few moments now to take the My Life Ladder™ Assessment in Appendix B.)

> "There is perhaps nothing worse than reaching the top of the ladder and discovering that you're on the wrong wall."
>
> —Joseph Campbell

Let's take a closer look at each rung:

Spirit

Spirit is the base of the ladder. When the spirit is strong and healthy, you can move with confidence to the next rungs. If however, you are not happy with yourself and not taking good care of your spirit, you can't fully give of yourself in your relationships with others.

The definition of spirit is a nonphysical part of a person that is the seat of emotions and character. It is the connection between body and soul. People engage their spirit in different ways. Some connect with their spirit by being in nature, meditating, practicing yoga, going to church, or holding deep conversations. It could be as simple as breathing.

- What matters most to you for tapping into your spirit?
- What allows you to connect with your spirit?
- What brings you peace?
- What brings you fulfillment?

Connecting with your spirit often requires slowing down and listening to your inner self. It's easy to focus only on what's urgent, which is why I fanatically schedule time to tap into my spirit and follow the wisdom in the downloads I receive. This guides my focus toward the truly important things or what matters most to me at the soul level.

There are five rungs to the ladder and, yet, if I have an issue in my life about community, it is all based on my spirit. If I have an issue with my craft, it is usually around the spirit. If there is an issue with relationships or me, it all starts with the foundation, which is spirit. It is very difficult, if not impossible, to resolve an issue without addressing this first rung of the ladder. Living and acting with an iMatter mindset starts with me honoring my spirit.

On the spirit rung, I look deeply into the core of my being, knowing that if I satisfy my soul's desires, I can be happy, more productive, and more present to be able to recognize and connect with the people who will love me and support me. Nurturing the spirit helps me define what I want from life and learn the lessons I am here to learn during this lifetime. Spirit comes first because a life without a sense of spirit is hardly living.

The things of the spirit are the things that give us energy and turn us back to the world with hope, love, and joy. For me, tapping into my spirit happens when I am driving with the windows down on a warm spring day, going for walks and being near water, watching an amazing sunset, practicing yoga, hiking in the mountains, engaging in deep conversations—anything where I am out of my head (and the chatter) and present in a state of being.

Health

As the vessel of the soul, the body is the means for achieving that which the soul desires. It makes sense to prioritize keeping the vessel in optimal working condition.

Again, think about what matters most to your health and physical well-being—is it food, water, sleep, exercise, sports, hiking, or perhaps something else? I want to be healthier and live a long life, so keeping my body nurtured with exercise or movement, nutritious foods, sea salt, water, and a good night's sleep is imperative.

You may say, as many do, "I don't have enough time to exercise," or "I can't go to bed earlier," or "Healthy food is too expensive."

My response is this: What do you want out of life? Do you think you can find fulfillment and enjoy your life if you haven't taken care of your body?

If you haven't already, I invite you to decide that your health matters to you and then focus on it. Achieving and maintaining good health is all about habits. Commit to a habit for thirty days and let it become a nurturing part of your life. Small changes like going to bed a little earlier or eating one healthy meal per day can make a big difference on this rung. (My wife has written five books and has a blog on the subject of healthy living and wellness. Learn more at APlaceToBe.com.)

Relationships

The key relationships in my life are the people I include on my team—the people closest to me. I trust the people within this circle of confidantes above all others. These are the people who matter most to me. I want to put energy into getting to know them in a richer way and sharing my authentic self with each of them. I am free to be myself with my team because we follow the Rules of Engagement and hold a safe space for each other. We may even share our Take 5 or go on retreats together.

I had to learn that I couldn't have *everyone* on my team. Instead, I had to consider who I trusted most and with whom I believed I could have a fulfilling, honest, and mutually rewarding experience. Then I worked on nurturing and improving those relationships.

I once worked with a young, successful executive who loved to party and enjoyed going to sporting events with his buddies. He insisted that partying was what mattered most on his spirit and relationship rungs. He believed his challenge was to convince his wife to stop complaining about his partying and appreciate what was important to him. I pushed him to be honest with himself and do what he had to do to live out what truly mattered most to him.

He may have been a big party guy, but he wasn't stupid. When he began to think through the life he really wanted, he realized that his wife and his relationship with her were more important to him than all his partying. He was brave enough to share his realization with her. He apologized, noting that even though he said she mattered most, he had not been acting like it in the way he chose to spend his time. They refocused their relationship and committed to spend more time having fun together because that was what truly mattered most.

Craft

There are jobs, there are careers, and then there is your craft, the one thing that you excel at above all others. Jobs pay you to do something that you may or may not care about. Careers consist of working at something you are probably pretty good at but still have room for growth. A craft is a skill, talent, or wisdom you use to learn and grow and that you *must* share with others. iMatter is my craft.

I learned about the concept of craft from *Inside the Actors Studio* with James Lipton. Mr. Lipton interviewed great actors to learn about their history, childhood, and upbringing to find out what types of struggles they had growing up. He brilliantly tied into some of their great roles and asked them if that upbringing helped them convey the emotions and feelings of that character in the movie. Many of the actors responded that absolutely it helped them tap into their character. It also helped them heal the wounds from their past.

My encouragement to you is to tap into where you may need and want to be healed, learn what you can, and then share that learning with others.

Your craft is your contribution to the world, part of the Great Gift you have to share with others. (If you aren't sure what your Great Gift is, don't worry! You'll discover that in the next chapter.) Ask yourself: Do you have a craft? What would it be? Can you be an authentic thought leader in that craft?

Doing my craft makes me whole. When I do it, I benefit others as well as myself. As I hone my craft, it contributes not only to my happiness and impact but also to my income. I believe the same will be true for you.

When you get to the place where you spend most of your time working within your passion, you will know you have found your craft. You will wake up each day excited by what you get to bring to the world.

Community

As you step into your greatness using your craft, it's natural to want to be of service and do something even greater for the world. That brings you up to the next rung on the ladder: Community.

On this rung, we donate or invest our time, money, or the skills that we've honed through our craft. We seek to use the influence we've achieved through building great relationships to do the world some good.

Community is the place we live and the place we give love. Your community might be a school, church, temple, favorite coffee shop, local library, neighborhood, city, or peer group. Community is the rung where what we give comes back tenfold in surprising ways, without expectation. We take care of one another. We take care of our world.

Many people want to feel that they are doing some good with their time on the planet but find it difficult to set aside enough time or cash to make a difference. Again, we're talking about the things that matter most. We're talking about living a great life.

Start small if you must. You have something you can give that can make a difference. One great place to start is within a community of peers (i.e., for your industry or current role in life). For me, my contribution to my peer community was starting The Visionary Forum™. I created space where kick-ass Visionary entrepreneurs could gather and learn from one another. We push each other to step into our greatness through community, safe space, and inspiration. Learn more at TheVisionaryForum.com.

Now that you understand each rung on the ladder, let's talk about what matters most to you. The next tool will help you define or refine what matters most to you.

iMatter Tool: The What Matters Most Realizer™

The What Matters Most Realizer helps you dig deeper into your soul and get clarity about what living your best life could look like. You can then fill out each rung of your Life Ladder—spirit, health, relationships, craft, and community—with the big values you want to build your life around. Going through the What Matters Most Realizer is like a mini boot camp for your soul! Take some time to work through the realizer tool now.

UNSCATTER THE CHATTER

SPIRIT

WHAT	WHY	NEXT STEPS

HEALTH

WHAT	WHY	NEXT STEPS

RELATIONSHIPS

WHAT	WHY	NEXT STEPS

CRAFT

WHAT	WHY	NEXT STEPS

THE WHAT MATTERS MOST REALIZER™ **⁑MATTER**

COMMUNITY

WHAT	WHY	NEXT STEPS

WHAT MATTERS MOST: THE BIG THINGS

WHAT	WHY	NEXT STEPS

WHAT MATTERS MOST: THE SMALL THINGS

WHAT	WHY	NEXT STEPS

THINGS TO LET GO OF

WHAT	WHY	NEXT STEPS

Many of my clients have been surprised in their iMatter Journey to discover that finding happiness and meaning in life isn't about doing more of something or doing something new and different. Most often it is about getting rid of some of the things that just don't matter most. It's about letting go. My experience is evidence of that.

Remember the old Bob, the one with that fully checked-off life list who got smacked around by the universe a bit? I cannot even compare the person I was then to the person I am today. I had no idea what mattered to me then. I didn't think to question what I was doing or why—or if it even mattered. Through my iMatter Journey, I have come to realize that living out what matters most to me has an impact. In fact, how I *think, act,* and *be* in my life as I step into my greatness has a ripple effect on the world around me.

Now that you have one piece of paper that lays out everything in life that matters most to you, take a look at your lifestyle. Are the things that matter most to you at the center of your life as you're living it today? Review your next steps and start taking action. What can you do right now that will bring you closer to what matters most? Do it—even if it's just to put a notice on your calendar or make a phone call to someone who's important to you.

As you use the What Matters Most Realizer tool as a filter, give yourself permission to say no to what doesn't matter most to you. Can you get rid of it or at least do less of it? Clearing up some of the clutter in your life frees you to enjoy what you love and make faster, more effective decisions regarding which walls you want to lean your ladder against next.

What about the walls?

Walls are the opportunities or relationships you're investing in. They can be impacted and supported by the rungs on your ladder. The stronger your ladder, the more discerning you will be of what wall to put it against.

If you lean your ladder against a wall, climb up it, and it's the right wall, fantastic! Stay there a while and enjoy the opportunity or relationship. If you climb up and discover the opportunity or relationship isn't right for you, as Campbell said, "Jump; it's not that far!" It is not a failure to jump from that wall. It may not have been the right time or the right opportunity, and that's okay. You've learned something and you've strengthened your ladder in the process.

Don't be afraid of discovering you're on the wrong wall. It's not as far back down to the ground as you think, and if your ladder is strong, you'll ascend the next wall easily and with joy. In my experience, most people don't find they need to abandon their career path or the community they are a part of so much as they need to reprioritize what matters to them about it.

My client Paul, for example, realized while he was on the mountain retreat with me that he wanted to say no to an opportunity. He had been focusing on increasing his status. By using these tools, he discovered he didn't care about status anymore. It no longer mattered to him.

At first, he thought the solution might be to cancel his country club membership. After some reflection, however, he realized it was his attitude about the country club he wanted to get rid of. He had long believed that he had to be competitive and act entitled to enjoy the club. He shifted his frustration and let go of the competition, what he thought other people thought about him, and how he thought he should be there. What mattered to him was the golf community and playing golf. When he realized status didn't matter, he was able to say no to being something he wasn't and simply enjoy the community as a golfer.

At iMatter, we say jump, strengthen your ladder, then find the most appropriate wall (for me, if it's not simple and peaceful, it's probably not the appropriate one). You might have to do it again later. Don't worry. Jumping is part of the iMatter Journey. Every time you jump, your ladder gets stronger.

Now that you've realized what matters most to you, let's focus the iMatter Legacy Lens on figuring out your *how* using the Lifetime Expander of Clarify Who You Are.

9

Who Am I?

Who am I?

Using the iMatter Journey, its tools, processes, and Think–Act–Be regularly in my life I have come to realize that I am a great father and husband, a Visionary entrepreneur, a community leader, an authentic thought leader, and a connector. Most importantly, I am me! iM!

Knowing who I am makes me confident about what I do and how I act. I can serve those who matter most to me by being my authentic self. I don't have to decide who I am when I show up in new settings; I'm always the same. This saves me so much stress.

For a long time, I questioned whether I was a good businessperson because I knew I was not a good manager. Then I met Gino Wickman in EO, and he became my EOS Implementer®. He helped me to see my role in my company as the Visionary and encouraged and equipped me to put structure around who we were as an organization and where we were going. I began to realize that I had a specific set of necessary business and leadership skills.

The more I owned my leadership style, the more my team saw how happy I was working from my Visionary space. My team found even more ways to help me stay in that space. I gave them permission to pull me back on track because the Visionary in me has the tendency to get distracted by a new idea every fifteen minutes! When I, a Visionary leader, am happy, I get out of my team's way, I drive more business, I solve problems more efficiently, and I don't become a bottleneck. Most importantly, I use my Great Gift to impact my clients, my team, my family, and the world. I realized that I could be myself at home and in business successfully and feel like I mattered in both worlds. It's a very good thing to know who you are and how you can make an impact on the world.

Lifetime Expander 4—Clarify Who You Are

Using the first three Lifetime Expanders, you've cleared away the clutter, and the real you is beginning to shine through. Are you beginning to feel more like *yourself*? I hope so! As you continue to move along in your iMatter Journey, it's essential to clarify who you are. When you know yourself, what matters to you, and where you excel, you have the power to make a meaningful and lasting impact on the world.

Your *how* is your Great Gift—the thing you do best and that brings you joy. When you are using your Great Gift, you easily slip into flow, that state of being in which you are fully present in the moment. Discovering my Great Gift was one of my most profound insights into clarifying who I am. It made me feel as if I could change the world.

Operating in my Great Gift looks like what some people will call being in the zone. Dan Sullivan, the founder of Strategic Coach®, calls something similar your Unique Ability®. I define your Great Gift as the essence of what you love to do and what you do best. It's what comes easy to you, feels natural, even magical! This is your gift to the world. When I'm using my Great Gift, I am loving life and teaching what I'm on this earth to teach. I know that my *how* makes a huge difference in the world. I was fortunate to find ways to live my Great Gift before I knew what it was.

> **Your Great Gift is the essence of what you love to do and what you do best.**

If you can name your Great Gift right away and are living it, congratulations! For some people, however, discovering a Great Gift may be a lifelong process. I find that I constantly refine the concept of my Great Gift as I discover and try new things.

Defining Your Great Gift™

To define my Great Gift, I started paying careful attention to what I loved to do, the things that excited me, and what I felt I was great at both at work and in my personal life. I asked myself, "What am I doing when I'm working in a state of inspired creative passion?"

After listing the activities that move me into flow, I looked for the common theme by considering how those things were similar or where they overlapped.

As you use the next two tools—the Who Am I Clarifier™ and the I Am Revealer™—you will discover your Great Gift, or at least part of it. Remember that you can refine and reassess. If you're anything like me, you may never find the whole answer because you are committed to continual growth and discovery.

iMatter Tools: The Who Am I Clarifier and the I Am Revealer

There are many ways to discover and understand who you are, including personality assessments that will give you letters and numbers and traits, for example. Some of these include the Kolbe A Index, DISC, and Myers-Briggs and Enneagram Assessments. All those are great if they help you understand more about yourself, and we use some of them with our coaching clients. Some people go on vision quests, spiritual journeys, or retreats. These are also excellent times of self-discovery, which is why we developed our retreat, Go to the Mountain (GoToTheMountain.com).

Aside from those tools and activities, we have created two iMatter tools to guide you as you seek to understand yourself with greater clarity. Remember, though, no matter what tool you are using, the answers are inside you.

The first tool we'll explore here delves into who you are. The Who Am I Clarifier™ walks you through a matrix of things you like or can't stand, fit your strengths or aren't good at, or that fit your strengths and you love! By reviewing the categories and, specifically, the "Things I Kick-Ass At and Love" category, you'll gain clarity on your Great Gift.

UNSCATTER THE CHATTER

WHEN PEOPLE THINK OF ME, THEY WOULD SAY:

WHAT	WHY	NEXT STEPS

WHEN I THINK OF MYSELF, I WOULD SAY:

WHAT	WHY	NEXT STEPS

THINGS I CAN'T STAND AND SUCK AT:

WHAT	WHY	NEXT STEPS

THINGS THAT FIT MY STRENGTHS, BUT I WOULD RATHER NOT DO:

WHAT	WHY	NEXT STEPS

BOB SHENEFELT

THINGS I LIKE AND AM NOT GOOD AT (HOBBIES):

WHAT	WHY	NEXT STEPS

THINGS THAT FIT MY STRENGTHS, AND I ENJOY:

WHAT	WHY	NEXT STEPS

THINGS THAT I KICK-ASS AT AND LOVE:

WHAT	WHY	NEXT STEPS

THINGS TO START DOING: THINGS TO STOP DOING:

After you've completed the Who Am I Clarifier, I encourage you to write themes on your Notes to Self page and then continue to work through the next tool: the I Am Revealer™. This tool helps you compare your self-concept to what others think of you. With this awareness, you'll discover where your strengths and passions lie.

The I Am Revealer clarifies and creates certainty as to who you are and how you impact others. You'll use it to affirm the "I Am" statements you've identified for your life. As you shift the conversation and turn other "Am I?" questions into "I Am" assertions, you'll get clear about what your Great Gift is and how you can share it with the world.

You can download these templates at iMatter.com/UnscatterTheChatter or join our online community at TheiMatterJourney.com.

BOB SHENEFELT

THE I AM REVEALER™   ᶦMATTER

WHAT FRUSTRATES ME

WHAT	WHY	NEXT STEPS

WHAT DO PEOPLE REALLY WANT

WHAT	WHY	NEXT STEPS

WHAT OTHERS WOULD SAY I'M HERE TO TEACH

WHAT	WHY	NEXT STEPS

MEETING/ENCOUNTERS WHEN I ROCKED

MEETING / ENCOUNTER	WHY	NEXT STEPS

UNSCATTER THE CHATTER

MEETING/ENCOUNTERS WHEN I DIDN'T ROCK

MEETING / ENCOUNTER	WHY	NEXT STEPS

WORDS ABOUT ME WHEN I AM ON

WORD	WHY	NEXT STEPS

HOW I FEEL WHEN I AM ON

FEELING	WHY	NEXT STEPS

I AM STATEMENT / GREAT GIFT

IDENTIFYING YOUR GREAT GIFT

As you work through these tools and the others throughout the iMatter Journey, you may notice that some words come to mind repeatedly. Those words show you what is important to you, how you are showing up, and how you are acting and being in life.

That has been true for me as well. In fact, ten words came up for me again and again:

1. Listen
2. Opportunity
3. Growth
4. Simplify
5. Connect
6. Inspire
7. Action
8. Greater
9. Future
10. Today

Based on these ten words, I have crafted a sentence describing my Great Gift: **I listen for opportunities for growth and to simplify, connect, and inspire action toward a greater future, today.**

I love those words. They speak to who I am and reveal my value to the world. I share them with my team so they know what I am about and can recognize opportunities for using my gift.

I've left some space for you to write your Great Gift statement at the end of this chapter. Once you've written it, I encourage you to share it with people you trust.

When I first shared my working draft with my wife, I didn't have the word *listen* in my statement. She pointed back to conversations I'd had with her and others and said, "When you listen, you are amazing." To be fair, her statement also recognized that I don't always listen. In her truth-telling, however, she pointed out a strength that I knew I wanted to harness and hone.

The same will likely be true for you. When you share your Great Gift statement with people you trust and who know you well, they will be able to point out words you may have left out or areas where you excel.

Next, let's jump into the *why* part of the iMatter Legacy Lens, through the Lifetime Expander, Follow Your North Star.

My Great Gift Statement

_____

_____

_____

10

What Guides You?

Here in the Northern Hemisphere, Polaris, or the North Star, is the brightest star in the sky. For centuries, sailors and explorers alike have used the North Star for navigation. The iMatter Journey relies on *your* North Star or your *why* to navigate through life in your journey of self-mastery. Your North Star guides the way toward greater purpose and peace. It is a vision—a beacon—that guides you in living out your legacy.

In Japan, this concept is referred to as *ikigai*, or a reason for being. One's *ikigai* lives inside the overlap of passion, mission, vocation, and profession. Once you know what it is, it becomes a guiding force for your life.

Lifetime Expander 5—Follow Your North Star

 Before you can follow your North Star, you've first got to find it. If you've done the work of realizing what matters most and clarifying who you are, you're well on your way. Discovering your Great Gift is also important because your Great Gift often points like a compass toward your North Star.

Through the tools such as the Take 5 Check-In as well as the What Matters Most Realizer, Who Am I Clarifier, and I Am Revealer, I noticed words, like *leader*, *entrepreneurial spirit*, *connection*, and *community* as recurring themes in my life. Not surprisingly, they are part of my North Star.

When I keep my North Star in view, it guides how I make decisions. It helps me determine which walls to lean my ladder against. It helps simplify making the decision to say yes or no to possibilities, opportunities, or relationships. I ask, *Is this in alignment with my North Star and what matters most to me on my Life Ladder?* If it's a yes, full speed ahead! If the answer is no, I know that going forward would be a waste of my precious time and energy.

By sharing my North Star with my team and giving them permission to remind me of it, I'm able to set myself up for further success toward living it. Sometimes they ask me, "If your North Star is *x*, why wouldn't you go do *y* to get you there?"

FOLLOWING MY NORTH STAR

It wasn't until I was deep into the final revisions on this book that I identified my North Star. For years, I've said that my North Star was to grow kids, grow Visionary entrepreneurs, and grow community. Those things are still integral to my life, but in the intensity of reflection that comes with writing a book, I realized that growing kids, growing entrepreneurs, and growing community is my *what*, not my why. My *why*—my North Star—is to elevate the entrepreneurial spirit through self-mastery and connection.

What is entrepreneurial spirit? To me, it represents independence and self-responsibility. It's the spirit that says, "I am not dependent on others. I am willing to take risks. I am willing to bet on myself and my life."

A person doesn't have to own a business to have the entrepreneurial spirit. So the kids I work with fit under the umbrella of my North Star—the self-mastery it takes to step into one's greatness and lead others, as well as the connection required.

Take my friend J.P. Hogan as an example of someone who is following his North Star. J.P. served for thirty years in the military and then spent another twenty in business. He built his life around service, but when he came through our iMatter coaching program, he realized he wanted to now serve his wife and family.

The iMatter Journey helped him see that he mattered and equipped him to define a vision for his life. He realized that what mattered most was his marriage, which led to making some changes in his life. He also discovered his North Star was growing leaders and giving back to his wife for the decades of support she had given him. He has now created an amazing home. His commitment to his wife, children, and grandchildren shine through as he works to grow leaders.

Your Guiding Light

My point in sharing my North Star and the journey it took to fully understand it is that even when we can't see our North Star, it is always there. Like the moon and all the other stars, they are there in the daytime, even though we can't see them. Our North Star continually guides and propels us (sometimes pushing us and at other times pulling us) toward living the legacy we want to leave.

Your North Star guides your actions, decisions, and relationships. If you think of your Great Gift as the value you create and what you enjoy sharing more than anything, your North Star tells you where to expend that energy and use that gift.

If you don't know yet what your North Star is, that's okay! You can start by reflecting on your ten keywords from the Who I Am Clarifier and the I Am Revealer. It can take time to figure out your North Star. It may even change as you learn, grow, and evolve.

We developed the following tools to help you find your North Star. The Connection Game™ is a fun way to start this discovery process. It helps you get to know yourself (and others) and learn what inspires you.

iMatter Tool: The Connection Game

The iMatter Journey is about understanding yourself—what brings you happiness, fulfillment, and joy for the adventure of life. The Connection Game is an entrée to a deep dive into knowing yourself and what inspires you in life to help you find your North Star.

UNSCATTER THE CHATTER

FAVORITE BOOKS

BOOK	WHY	NEXT STEPS

FAVORITE MOVIES

MOVIE	WHY	NEXT STEPS

FAVORITE CHARACTERS

CHARACTER	WHY	NEXT STEPS

FAVORITE SONGS

SONG	WHY	NEXT STEPS

BOB SHENEFELT

THE CONNECTION GAME™   **iMATTER**

FAVORITE THINGS

THING	WHY	NEXT STEPS

FAVORITE PLACES

PLACE	WHY	NEXT STEPS

FAVORITE MEMORIES

MEMORY	WHY	NEXT STEPS

FAVORITE SUCCESS STORIES

SUCCESS STORY	WHY	NEXT STEPS

After you complete the Connection Game exercise, review your answers and think about why they are important to you.

What do these favorites ignite in you?

Do they bring you closer to what you are passionate about?

Do they provide clues to your purpose or North Star for your own life?

We often learn by observing other people's lives, which can help offer us new perspectives about life and meaning in life. With that in mind, consider sharing this tool with others. Bring it to your next dinner party and learn what values or themes show up for your friends and family. Learning more about what inspires others can help you feel more connected to them (and yourself). As you feel more connected, it reminds you that you matter, you have something great to share with the world, and it helps you home in on your North Star.

Here's one example of how this works: The people and characters that emerged in my answers during the Connection Game gave me insight into myself and my North Star. I noticed consistent themes that the characters shared, including humor, community, doing the right thing, serving, and integrity. The following people or characters are related to things that matter to me as well as my why and my purpose for being:

- **Bill Murray**—I admire people who maintain a sense of humor. Murray has the gift of finding the light in the dark and flipping on the switch for the rest of us.
- **George Bailey**—*It's a Wonderful Life* is possibly my favorite movie. I think the old Bob could identify quite closely with George at the beginning of the film—doing the right thing but feeling unappreciated. I've learned along with George that being a

good person and doing your best carry weight into every aspect of my life, including the lives I touch. Our actions cause ripples, like a pebble tossed in a pond.

- **Bugs Bunny**—From the time I was a small child, I just got Bugs. He calls out the other characters on their stuff, puts bullies in their place, and does it all with a fun, cool attitude full of humor. Bugs was also a reminder of time with my dad, connecting and laughing together.
- **Franklin D. Roosevelt**—FDR was strong in the face of adversity and a servant leader. He knew the value of serving and changing the world for others, not himself.

See an example of my Connection Game at iMatter.com/ UnscatterTheChatter.

iMatter Tool: The North Star Identifier™

Another tool to help you find your purpose and passion in life is the North Star Identifier. It starts with a question many people shy from: What is your desired eulogy? Take a deep breath and give this tool a chance with an open heart and open mind.

Thinking about death can bring a lot of meaning to your life. Imagine that you could look down from heaven and listen to what people say about you at your funeral. What would you want to hear? What did you accomplish? What kind of person were you? What are the favorite memories your friends and family are sharing about you? What keywords keep coming up?

Write down what you hope people will say. If it's not what you think they would say if you passed on tomorrow, then you'll have some great insights you can use to fill in some of the other sections on the worksheet or to add to your Notes to Self page.

Remember the story I told about my brother-in-law? When he died at the young age of twenty-three, he had already made a powerful impression on a great many people. His life touched mine. The way he was remembered by others pushed me further in my journey to live an authentic life and leave a great legacy.

His funeral, and my dad's, were what made me think of what I wanted the guests at my own funeral to say, and as a result, I made some changes in my life. I reflect on this tool often to ensure that I'm leaving the legacy I want. I use the North Star Identifier tool quarterly (and sometimes more often) so I can write down everything I want people to say in my eulogy. I use it as motivation to share my Great Gift and follow my North Star as much as possible.

What do you think your kids, family, and colleagues would say about you now if you died? It may sound a bit morose, but this isn't about focusing on death; it's about focusing on the life you want to live. Don't take for granted the short time you have here on earth. There may be plenty of time to accomplish something great, but there's no time to waste!

Sometimes, your North Star can seem elusive. Don't worry if there is a struggle in finding it. In doing the work and using the iMatter Journey, truly implementing all the mindsets and tools we've learned so far, your North Star will ultimately reveal itself.

When it does, you won't be able to miss it.

BOB SHENEFELT

DESIRED EUOLOGY

IF YOU DIED TOMORROW, WHAT MEMORIES WILL BE SHARED?

WHAT	WHY	NEXT STEPS

IF YOU DIED TOMORROW, WHAT HAVEN'T YOU FINISHED?

WHAT	WHY	NEXT STEPS

WHAT DO YOU WANT FOR YOUR KIDS?

WHAT	WHY	NEXT STEPS

UNSCATTER THE CHATTER

IF YOU HAVE A YEAR TO LIVE, WHAT MATTERS MOST?

WHAT	WHY	NEXT STEPS

IF YOU HAVE 10 YEARS TO LIVE, WHAT MATTERS MOST?

WHAT	WHY	NEXT STEPS

WHAT WOULD YOUR FAMILY/FRIENDS SAY YOU ARE MOST PASSIONATE ABOUT?

WHAT	WHY	NEXT STEPS

WHAT IS YOUR NORTH STAR (YOUR WHY)?

Remember—you are not alone on this journey. Be sure to check out our self-guided journey and iMatter Community at TheiMatterJourney.com to take a deeper dive into yourself through the process, or if you want more hands-on guided support, we have iMatter coaches who can support you through our 90-day Enlightened Visionary Bootcamp.

Living through the iMatter Legacy Lens

Finding clarity is an ongoing process. As you continue to step into your greatness, your thinking will change. You will grow, gain new wisdom, and evolve into a more authentic you. On this journey, be intentional about continually relying on Think-Act-Be. The way you *think* affects how you *act*, which shapes the way you choose to *be*. It is your *be*ing that enables you to *have* and *do* what you envision in your life.

Remember how I said I would keep sharing my personal journey? Well, something life changing happened while I was writing this book.

In February of 2020, Sheryl and I went to the mountain for a retreat for our twentieth anniversary and to do another deep dive into the iMatter Journey. We went through the tools together and shared and talked and laughed and drank a lot of wine. It was a lovely time of connection to ourselves and each other. It was an important time for me because I finally owned the belief that I am successful. I have built a great f'ing life for myself, and I love it. We celebrated the present and dreamed of all the wonderful things we would accomplish in 2020 and beyond.

Then the pandemic hit, and it felt like nobody could dream anymore. Everything was about death tolls, hospital beds, and economies grinding to a halt. Some of the old demons returned—those bullying voices and doubting chatter filled my head. I grew impatient and frustrated that I still didn't have my book out and that we didn't have the material I wanted online available yet. Meanwhile, constant turmoil dominated the news. I thought this was a valley in my life, but little did I know.

Then came 2021, and life brought me to my knees. In fact, it paralyzed me. I woke up at 3:00 a.m., my head was numb, my left arm was not working very well, and I wasn't even sure I could speak enough to tell Sheryl to call 9-1-1.

It turns out that I was suffering a stroke. Luckily, I got to the hospital in time, and the medical team treated me quickly.

I tell people, "Don't wait for a heart attack or divorce to wake up," and here it was happening to me in the form of a stroke. Fear took over as I faced my death—fear that I wasn't leaving a legacy, I was letting my kids down, letting my wife down. *It's too early*, I told myself. *It can't be my time yet. I have so much more to teach.* While I lay there, I started to have a conversation with God.

"Is my life over?" I asked.

A resounding "no" reassured me.

"Is it because I still have more to teach?" I asked.

Again, the answer was, "No."

God went on to say, "You still have more to *learn*."

Whoa—that was a wake-up call for me. My breakdown became another breakthrough to not only practice what I teach but also to be open to learning beyond what I already *think* I know.

In other words, I'm still very much on this iMatter Journey—and grateful to be! I have to constantly Shift the Conversation on my inner chatter and Flip It to realize that, all things considered, I am still living a *great* life, and, hey, the book is finally finished!

The stroke reminded me of a truth I already knew: Legacy is meant to be lived. What matters most is the legacy you *live in the moment* each and every day as you choose to continue to step into your greatness with conviction and trust the adventure of life. It was this reminder that birthed another Lifetime Expander: Live Your Legacy, *Now*. This is a lesson in being open to possibilities and allowing life to unfold. To help others and myself, we use a tool called My iMpact Planner™. My iMpact Planner gives you a place to visualize what you identify using the iMatter tools. Similar in purpose to a vision board or dashboard for your life, the planner keeps your intentions and what's most important to you front and center. It also guides you as you assess the strength of the rungs on our Life Ladder each quarter. Let's look at it now as we begin the third step of the iMatter Journey: Confidence.

PART 5

Confidence

The third step on the iMatter Journey of self-mastery is confidence. The goal is to live and love your life with conviction and the deep inner knowing that *you matter*. In this step, we'll focus on two Lifetime Expanders: Live Your Legacy, *Now* and Be, Regardless.

Here in Part 5, we'll delve into how you can maintain your new operating system or new way of viewing *and* doing life as you implement the iMatter tools and practices as daily, weekly, and quarterly habits. *Using the tools* can ultimately help you continue to unscatter the chatter, elevate your mind, and make a huge impact in your life and the world around you.

CONFIDENCE

COMMUNITY

CRAFT

RELATIONSHIPS

HEALTH

SPIRIT

11

Know and Act Like You Matter

onfidence. What does that word mean to you?

To me, it means that I believe and act like iMatter. When I have confidence, I boldly step into my greatness. I have the conviction to continue to act on the insights I have obtained thus far while being open to new possibilities for growth and enlightenment. I move with confidence toward my goals of being present, making choices in alignment with What Matters Most on My Life Ladder, sharing and giving from a place of strength, using my Great Gift, and *living* my legacy in alignment with my North Star.

Lifetime Expander 6—Live Your Legacy, *Now*

Taking a journey like climbing a mountain (literally or figuratively) requires strategic footwork and an action plan. Similarly, the Live Your Legacy, *Now* Lifetime Expander encourages us to take inspired action toward the life we desire most.

The tool in this chapter—My iMpact Planner—will guide you to tap into your inner wisdom and remind you to choose to Live Your Legacy, *Now*. It will help you stay true to your North Star, day after day, week after week, quarter after quarter, and year after year. As you consciously choose to live and love your life (the definition of true self-mastery—iM!), you become even more confident in the knowledge that you matter.

> "The best way to predict the future is to create it."
>
> —Abraham Lincoln

iMatter Tool: My iMpact Planner

All of the iMatter tools in this book come together so you can create what we call My iMpact Planner. As you can see, I altered the first two letters of impact to emphasize the iM. The self-mastery (iM) of living and being *you* combined with the intentionality of creating your own reality or iMpact in the world. This tool gives you a snapshot vision for your life and the legacy you want to live right *now*. My encouragement is to use My iMpact Planner to keep a pulse on your life and your continued progress on your iMatter Journey.

My iMpact Planner is a simple, one-page document that outlines your plan for the next ninety days.

- It keeps your iMatter Legacy Lens focused sharply on your what, how, and why.

- It keeps tabs on the wisdom that comes through using your Take 5 Check-In, 3-3-1, and Notes to Self tools.
- As you look at the key areas of your Life Ladder, My iMpact Planner will enable you to live with intention and purpose.
- You'll regularly evaluate and honor what matters most to you. (Remember, you can't focus on everything. Focus on what's most important to you and permit yourself not to stress about the rest.)
- And it will keep your Great Gift and North Star in front of you like a compass guiding you on your journey.

Using this tool at the start of each quarter gives me a chance to contemplate the past quarter and assess where I am, my successes, and the lessons I've learned. I use this information and the knowledge of what and who matters most to me to determine what new goals I want to set for the next quarter and consider which walls I want to lean my ladder against.

Schedule at least two hours total each quarter to update your iMpact Planner. You may be thinking, *Oh great, another two hours I have to fit into my already busy life.* To that I say, *You matter!* I know you will find a great return on the investment of time you take to plan a productive, meaningful, and *fun* ninety days.

Find a space where you can contemplate deeply, where you will not be disturbed or distracted. Then get comfortable, take a deep breath, and clarify your plan with confidence.

MY iMPACT PLANNER™

DATE: _____ QTR: _____

NORTH STAR (WHY):
_____
_____
_____
_____

LIFE LADDER (WHAT):
_____
_____
_____

GREAT GIFT (HOW):
_____
_____
_____

TOP 3 WALLS FOR THE QUARTER

1:

2:

3:

WHO MATTERS MOST (TOP 10/TEAM)

_____ _____
_____ _____
_____ _____
_____ _____
_____ _____

IM STATEMENTS:
_____
_____
_____
_____
_____

How to Complete Your iMpact Planner

Step 1: Pull out your answers to the iMatter tools (Take 5 Check-In, 3-3-1, What Matters Most Realizer, Who Am I Clarifier, I Am Revealer, Connection Game, North Star Identifier, and Notes to Self page).

Step 2: My North Star

What is your why? What brings you passion in life? This is your guiding light, and you want to read and know it every time you look at your iMpact Planner so you can continue to *be* it. Your North Star Identifier will help you with this step.

Step 3: What Matters Most?

Ask: Right now, right here, what are the top three things that matter most to me this quarter? Write down your answers. This is a great time to go back through the What Matters Most Realizer. Sometimes your answer will change!

---

iMatter Tool: My Life Ladder Assessment

Another way to gain clarity for what matters most during the next ninety days is to take the My Life Ladder Assessment. This assessment will give you clarity and confidence regarding where to focus your energy.

The twenty questions of the My Life Ladder Assessment help you assess the strength of the rungs of your ladder, what and who matters most to you, and identify which ones need more focus. You'll find more about the assessment in Appendix B, on page 181.

Step 4: My Great Gift

Write down your best version of your Great Gift (your how). Don't worry if it's different from last quarter's Great Gift; this is a journey of discovery! Ask yourself what you love and what you are great at. Look back at your Who Am I Clarifier and I Am Revealer to help you complete this step.

Step 5: Top Three Walls

What are the top three walls (goals, opportunities, or relationships) you want to devote your time and energy to this quarter? These are things that if you accomplish, focus on, or nurture them, you will ensure progress toward your vision.

Step 6: Who Matters Most (Your Top Ten or Your Team)

Take a look at the people who surround you—your wife, partner, Integrator®, family members, and friends. Who do you trust? Who speaks the truth to you? Who shares your values? Who do you share your 3-3-1 and Take 5 with? Put the statement out to the universe that if you were to surround yourself with individuals who will hold you accountable, you would be on track toward living a great life.

Relationships require a lot of energy. Recognize where you spend your energy and refocus it on those people who matter the most.

Step 7: I Am (iM!)

Write down some important iM statements. You can return to these truths for strength and clarity throughout the month. These statements usually reflect emotional states or personal growth goals. They won't necessarily be measurable as they are more about shifting your consciousness. Think of them like affirmations and a way to keep your mind elevated and above the chatter that keeps you scattered, out of control, and out of the flow. Your iM statements keep you in the flow of being *you*.

Once you've completed your iMpact Planner, let it sit for twenty-four hours, then revisit it and revise if necessary.

Step 8: Share Your iMpact Planner

Here comes one last challenging part: Share your iMpact Planner with your team. Remember, any goal you write down and then share has a much greater chance of coming to fruition.

Sure, it can be awkward and scary the first time, but it's worth asking for feedback and support from others. You'll quickly see the advantages as your community rallies around you to help you achieve your goals and be who you are.

Remember John, who shifted the conversation in his head about his professional success? In our time working together, I decided to challenge him to share his iMpact Planner with his teenage sons.

"But then they might realize that their dad doesn't have a clue!" he objected.

I tried not to laugh too hard. "They're teenagers, John. They already think you don't have a clue!"

By sharing his iMpact Planner with them, becoming vulnerable, and showing them what matters most to him, John let his sons understand him at a deeper level, and they all grew closer. His younger son noticed that music was a value, and he helped John connect his phone to his car radio so he could listen to music on his way to work instead of the news.

Another client of mine decided to emphasize the spirit rung of his Life Ladder because he felt that part of his life had been lacking. In fact, he thought he wasn't a spiritual person at all. I knew within moments of meeting him that he was one of the most spiritual people I would ever know, but the noise of his life and society had blinded him to that part of himself.

He set a goal in his iMpact Planner to define spirituality for himself, then shared it with his in-laws. That got his father-in-law intrigued, and they talked for hours about the subject. They may not have solved anything that night. Still, that conversation created a stronger relationship between them and built a lot of trust. It was a safe space to hear himself think and figure some big things out.

Use the Tools

With My iMpact Planner in place, you have a central hub that connects the big picture values of your Life Ladder and the vision of your North Star with your day-to-day concerns in your Take 5 Check-In and 3-3-1.

Throughout the quarter, take stock of your iMpact Planner each week as you do your Take 5 Check-In.

- Are the important things still the important things?
- Have you accomplished what you listed for your walls?
- Are you living into your "iM" statements?
- Are you following your North Star?
- Are you Living Your Legacy, *Now*?

Making the tools part of your life and sharing your own iMpact Planner and keeping it up to date can help you make decisions about your life and continuously Think–Act–Be, from the iMatter mindset. This has helped me to unscatter the chatter and keep tapping into my own inner wisdom over the years when doubt and fear were holding me back.

One example of how My iMpact Planner keeps me focused is several years ago when my kids were home from school for a snow day. One of my personal house rules is that if the kids have a snow day, the parents have a snow day. I had just zipped them up in their gear, and we were about to go out to play when I got a phone call from a former EO friend. He asked me to come back on the board as forum chair. My immediate answer was, "No way, I can't commit to that."

That afternoon, I mentioned the call to my wife. I even added that I was proud I was learning to say *no*.

Sheryl paused for a moment and asked thoughtfully, "But isn't that part of what matters most to you? 'Leading other visionaries and giving back to peer groups in your community' are key portions of your Life Ladder and are front and center on your iMpact Planner. It seems to me that this wall or opportunity might be appropriate for you."

She was right, of course. I was too caught up in going to play with my kids to see it (although that did matter most right then). I am grateful to have someone on my team who can steer me back on course when choosing my next right step.

Another time, I got a call from my children's school asking if I would consider becoming the PTA president. PTA? Me? Definitely not. However, the North Star I had on my iMpact Planner at the time reminded me that I wanted to grow kids, grow communities, and grow entrepreneurs. After some thought, I realized that wall was worth my time and attention. Imagine what I could do to influence the curriculum. The idea of holding events to foster a new generation of entrepreneurs who start out knowing what matters most to them inspired me.

I became president, created a great board, and added real value by using my Great Gift to follow my North Star. I can still see the ripples of the pebbles I tossed into that pond flowing into iMatter for Kids™, the non-profit organization we created to help kids know they matter and to be who they are. The kids experienced amazing growth and breakthroughs. With their high school mentors, they used the iMatter Journey and its tools to step into their greatness. As they learned with wonder and openness, those children became mentors for their peers and even to their parents.

My iMpact Planner helps make your mark on the world by being unapologetically *you*—even in the face of fear, adversity, or judgment. As you Follow Your North Star, share your Great Gift, and choose which walls to lean your Life Ladder against, you will grow in the confidence that *you matter.*

Please, don't wait until it's too late. Live Your Legacy, *Now.*

12

Be Who You Are

Self-mastery is an ongoing journey of exploration and growth through commitment *and* clarity *and* confidence. It's about the *and*! It's the wisdom of iMatter.

When we choose to Think-Act-Be and live in the harmony of iM, we experience the magic and joy of being who we are. Life becomes a daring adventure!

On adventurous journeys, there will be valleys and summits—challenges that take us to the depths and moments of bliss and flow in which we *know* we are exactly who and where we are meant to be. The threat of the difficulties we are sure to face, however, must never prevent us from showing up and living with passion today—right *now*. We must press forward, grow, and choose to *be*.

As Neale Donald Walsh explained in his books *Conversations with God*, every choice is rooted in either fear or love. To Be, Regardless is to choose love.

Lifetime Expander 7—Be, Regardless

 Of all the mantras I can live out each day, I've realized that one of the greatest is to Be, Regardless. That is, to be present in my greatness and my truth and in the *now* moment, regardless of what else comes at me.

Like most entrepreneurs, I regularly find myself caught up in my business, personal obligations, health concerns, cashflow worries, family time, and more. It's easy to get overwhelmed. The key to find joy in it all is to *stop doing and start being*.

Love, life, magic, joy—it all starts with me and my choice to Be, Regardless. The fears of success, or putting myself out there, and concerns about *having* and *doing* diminish when I focus on simply *being*.

For me, to "Be, Regardless" means . . .

- I am focused on what and who matters most.
- I am present.
- I am aware of the synchronicity of thoughts and encounters.
- I am going with the flow of life with an open heart, open mind, and open palms.
- I am living in the iM state of self-mastery with Commitment, Clarity, and Confidence.

If you're going to be anything today, *Be, Regardless*. Use I Am statements to anchor and affirm your being present, aware, and open in the now moment. As you integrate the Be–Do–Have mindset into your life, you will repeatedly come back to Think-Act-Be. This is what gives you the power to *be*—to live in the harmony and power of iM self-mastery and the iMatter mindset. Choosing to Be, Regardless is to mindfully, moment by moment unscatter the chatter.

There is a great word I would like to share with you that I often use in my iM or affirmation statements. This word reminds me to have confidence and courage to stay in the flow with palms and heart open and continue to Be, Regardless.

Imperturbable.

What is imperturbable? This word means "unable to be upset or excited." I cannot be perturbed, steady as she goes.

One of the times this word really resonated with me most was while on a retreat in the mountains in Colorado with my entrepreneur forum. We'd had a wonderful dinner with great wine and great conversation. We were at about 11,000 feet in front of the Coors Mountain. (Yes, they literally trademarked the mountain.) When we came out of the lodge, we looked up and saw billions of stars, and I fell to the ground in awe. It was one of the most amazing things I've ever seen. My forum mate Curt said, "This is imperturbable."

At that moment, the word resonated with me in this deep sense that I could not be shaken. To see the vastness of the world and know that I am a part of it—I cannot be removed from it.

iM iMperturbable!

Although my part may be small, I am indeed part of this amazing, massive structure of the universe. I am here, and I have a place in it. That starry night showed me the meaning of what it means to be imperturbable and to feel the power of living in harmony with and standing in the truth of iM—iMatter!

PART 6

Enlightenment

Every time I experience the power of the iMatter tools, I feel re-energized, full of joy, and closer to my true self. I see the world around me like a child does, with excitement and wonder. To keep this feeling going, I use the tools regularly. This discipline builds confidence and proves to others and myself that I am dependable. It shows that I am staying true to my commitments to myself. When I make time for the daily, weekly, and quarterly rituals, I act like iMatter and tap into my inner genius. To me, this harmony and truth feels like a spiritual high or enlightenment.

You may be feeling the same right now.

Although you've completed the three steps of Commitment, Clarity, and Confidence, this is not the end of your iMatter Journey. Just like your iPhone needs updates on an ongoing basis, the iMatter Journey, your unique operating system, needs regular updates as well. What follows will help you maintain the life and enlightenment you've worked so intentionally to experience.

13

The Adventure Begins

This isn't the end of your iMatter adventure; it's just the beginning.

At this point, you are either exhausted or feel like you've got the world on a string, which is why I want to give you the best piece of inspiration I have: *You are not alone!* You are blessed throughout your journey to have people who can help you along the way.

Remembering that you matter seems like a simple task. Let's be honest, though, committing to oneself, to enlightenment, and to self-mastery isn't always easy.

This journey began with the encouragement to say to yourself, "I matter." iMatter.

I matter enough to invest in time for me. I matter enough to do the work. iMatter.

The truth is, even though I know iMatter, I must recommit regularly to the journey. I must continue to get to know myself. The more I do that, the more inspirations, thoughts, and visions come to me. They may be my own. They may be from my father who passed away years ago. They may be from God. I have no idea where they originate exactly, but I do know that when I connect with myself, take a deep breath, and step into those ideas and visions for my future, it is a wondrous place to be.

I have all the answers *inside*, and I know I am not alone.

Implementing iMatter into Your Life

I've thrown a lot at you in this book. It's important you don't think you need to master the use of every Lifetime Expander and iMatter tool today. The time to start is *now*, yes, but you can start the journey of self-mastery just one step at a time. Today, commit to taking your next step into your greatness. Self-mastery is about the journey, not the destination. Keep saying this over and over, like a mantra.

Add the tools into your life one by one. Use them regularly to create habits and rituals that become part of your rhythm. Start with adding the 3-3-1 into your day and do that for a couple of weeks. Next, find someone or a group or team to share the 3-3-1 tool with and discuss the experience (using the Rules of Engagement, of course). Then add the Take 5 Check-In at the beginning of your week. Look for ways to Shift the Conversation or Flip It during your day. Each time you use one of these tools, you'll notice where you spend your time and whether it is what you would *like* to spend your time on. Are they *have* tos or *love* tos?

Then you can begin the deeper work of the journey into the legacy you want to live by realizing What Matters Most (your Life Ladder), Clarifying Who You Are (your Great Gift), and Following Your North Star (your purpose or why). Commit to integrating the Lifetime Expanders and the iMatter tools into your life as you continue to evolve and expand into yourself fully. Keep imagining and improving so you can impact the moment.

Over several quarters, you will see that as you elevate your mind—you are nicer to yourself and others, you can depend on yourself more, and you are acting like you matter and being who you are. Making choices will become easier because you will be free to be yourself and say no to things that don't move you in the direction you want to go.

I've laid this out as a system that takes you from here to there. However, iMatter is not about the destination—that is why we call it a journey. It's a way of life, it's a mindset, it's a way to *be*. It is the realization that life's answers and joy come from within that transforms the world and ushers us into the wisdom age. *That's* the iMatter Revolution!

Your iMatter Journey will take time. Start where you are and take the first step into your greatness.

The time is *now*, and the power is *you*.

Closing Thoughts:
The Mountain Is Inside You

On my life's journey, I've climbed many mountains, both literal and figurative. I've dream-walked with my astrologer, journeyed with shamans, and even walked on fire. I've taken many personal, couples, and forum retreats. I've watched the sunrise and sunset over the mountains, seen many rainbows, and realized what my life could look like if I were just bold enough to embrace it.

Mountains symbolize many things: conquering, overcoming an issue, hard work, willpower, and transcending petty circumstances. Mountains are often thought to contain divine inspiration and are the focus of pilgrimages and both physical and spiritual elevation.

For some believers, the top of the mountain is the closest we can get to God. It is beyond the standard human experience and puts us as close as possible to the sky and heaven.

The first time I went to my (literal) mountain, it was to figure out what the heck I was doing with my life. I can't say why I chose this particular place; in all truth, I'd say it chose me. I learned later that there is a vortex in the mountains of Colorado, a measurable spike of energy that comes up out of the earth. It is transformational. When I am there, I feel cleansed, calmed, and energized. The physical mountain, however, is only a vehicle for unlocking what was already within me.

The truth is, I don't need to be on a physical mountain to feel that way. I carry that energy around *inside me*. I can choose to *go to the mountain within* any time.

The mountain within changes my perspective. It allows me to check in and get in touch with myself physically, mentally, and spiritually. As I continue to learn, share, and teach, the mountain within is a place where I can take time and be with my thoughts.

To me, the mountain symbolizes self-mastery—the greatest achievement we can reach as humans. It's the place where we function as our highest and best selves. The mountain is a manifestation of living one's best life.

Everyone has a mountain: It could be a hot bath or a northern Michigan beach or a drive on a beautiful night with the windows down and the music loud. The mountain is the place where you can just *be*.

You might be thinking, *Bob, I have no mountain; what are you talking about?* I'm going to tell you a secret: You are on your way up the mountain now. Each step you take, each decision you make is one step closer. It's like the old joke:

How do you eat an elephant? One bite at a time. The mountain is the same. Just one step at a time, one inch closer to the reason, the meaning, the purpose of your being.

I have a friend who frames her life around the mantra, "My feet have brought me here." It's her way of accepting that she is an active participant in her destination despite the things that may seem out of her control. When aligned with what matters most (our Life Ladder), the choices we make (walls of our life) take us to where we need to be.

When I need a wake-up call or an instant snap to being present, I say aloud, "Go to the mountain!" Sometimes, I say it like a mantra to elevate my mind, imagine myself on the mountain, and tap into the clarity I receive while I am there.

You can do the same.

As I write the last words of this book, I face my next step. I know the answers are inside me. Just as your answers are within you. The lessons we learn about ourselves in our unique journeys will expand and evolve as we do. My hope is that every step brings us closer to what matters to us personally *now*. Even so, I know that life happens; valleys happen. When they do, let us be confident enough to commit again to finding a clear vision for the path ahead.

Remember, we are on a journey. Even self-mastering and reaching the mountain within is not a final destination. What feels like the end is only the beginning.

What's Next?

When I began writing this book, I was inspired by Dad's Top Ten Life Lessons to share ten principles for living a great f'ing life. We came up with five Lifetime Expanders and agreed that was enough for this book—for the beginning of the journey.

Life had other ideas, though. Right when we thought the book was complete, having a stroke gave us the insight for two more: Live Your Legacy, *Now* and Be, Regardless.

The ink isn't even dry at the printing presses, and I'm already forming ideas about what's next—what will unfold in the next book and the next leg of the journey and learning my next Lifetime Expander to share with the world. I know that personally, for the next season of my life, what matters most to me is my health (Yes, I'm listening!) and community. I want to honor where I've been and honor the stroke as a wake-up call to not waste one precious moment of my life. Part of what brings joy and richness to my life is being with like-minded Visionary entrepreneurs. That's where community comes into play. I've found a wall to lean My Life Ladder on and have already started the climb to creating a safe space for where Visionaries on this journey of enlightenment can gather, share wisdom, and grow together. I truly hope you will be a part of it! To learn more, see the back pages of this book or visit iMatter.com.

What about you? Are you committed to your iMatter Journey? Will you use the Lifetime Expanders and iMatter tools to find clarity about who you are and what matters most to you? Will you choose to live with the confidence that *you matter*?

I certainly hope so. I'm so proud of you for embarking on this journey toward self-mastery—to iM!

Wherever you are, take the next step, do the next right thing, and continue growing and expanding. If your Life Ladder is leaning against a wall that isn't right for you, as Joseph Campbell said, "Jump, it's not that far."

176

Resources

- Step into Your Greatness and Live a Great F'ing Life: iMatter.com
- The iMatter Success System: TheiMatterJourney.com
- 90-Day Enlightened Visionary Bootcamp: iMatter.com
- Experiential Retreat of Commitment, Clarity, Conviction: GoToTheMountain.com
- The Hub for All Things Visionary: TheVisionaryForum.com
- Where Visionaries Connect: TheVisionarySummit.com

Additional Reading at iMatter.com/resources

3 Fables about the iMatter Journey, The Will Book Series:

- *What Matters Most: The Story of Will*
- *That Was Then, This is Now: The Clarity of Will*
- *If it Were Up to Me: The Legacy of Will*

APPENDIX A

Overview of the iMatter Journey

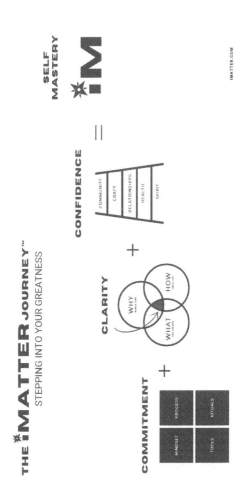

THE ✳iMATTER JOURNEY™
STEPPING INTO YOUR GREATNESS

CLARITY
WHY · HOW · WHAT

+

COMMITMENT
MINDSET · PROCESS · TOOLS · RITUALS

+

CONFIDENCE
COMMUNITY · CRAFT · RELATIONSHIPS · HEALTH · SPIRIT

=

SELF MASTERY
✳iM

IMATTER.COM

THE IMATTER JOURNEY™

		LIFETIME EXPANDERS	TOOLS
STEP 1	COMMITMENT	1. CREATE GREAT RELATIONSHIPS	The Rules of Engagement, The Take 5 Check-In, The 3-3-1
		2. CHOOSE YOUR ATTITUDE	Shift the Conversation, Flip It, Throw That Sh*t in the Fire
STEP 2	CLARITY	3. REALIZE WHAT MATTERS MOST	My Life Ladder, The What Matters Most Realizer
		4. CLARIFY WHO YOU ARE	The Who Am I Clarifier, The I Am Revealer
STEP 3	CONFIDENCE	5. FOLLOW YOUR NORTH STAR	The Connection Game, The North Star Identifier
		6. LIVE YOUR LEGACY, NOW	My iMpact Planner, My Life Ladder Assessment
		7. BE, REGARDLESS	Rituals of using The Think - Act - Be Process and Tools

		RITUALS	TOOLS
MAINTENANCE	ON GOING JOURNEY	DAILY	The 3-3-1 and Rules of Engagement
		WEEKLY	The Take 5 Check-In
		QUARTERLY	My iMpact Planner, My Life Ladder Assessment
		ANNUALLY—DEEP DIVE	My Life Ladder, The What Matters Most Realizer, The Who Am I Clarifier, The I Am Revealer, The Connection Game, The North Star Identifier
		AD-HOC / TROUBLESHOOTING	Shift the Conversation, Flip It, Throw That Sh*t in the Fire

APPENDIX B

The iMatter Tools

All of the iMatter tools are available at iMatter.com/
UnscatterTheChatter. There you can download printable
copies or fillable PDF versions of the forms and find completed examples.

- iMatter Rules of Engagement
- Take 5 Check-In
- Notes to Self Tool
- 3-3-1
- Shift the Conversation
- Flip It
- Throw That Sh*t in the Fire
- What Matters Most Realizer
- Who Am I Clarifier
- I am Revealer
- Connection Game
- North Star Identifier
- iMpact Planner
- My Life Ladder Assessment

Bonus iMatter Tool: The My Life Ladder Assessment

In Chapter 8, Expand Your Impact, I touched on the My
Life Ladder concept. Now, I'm going to teach you a powerful
practice that I complete at least quarterly to gain awareness

and perspective on where I'm at for each of the five rungs of My Life Ladder: spirit, health, relationships, craft, and community. This assessment also helps me fill out the What Matters Most part of my iMpact Planner. With it, I am able to stay focused on where I want to grow, expand, and evolve.

Recall that My Life Ladder shows what matters most to you. Whether you are aware of it or not, there may be rungs of your Life Ladder that have weak spots. Maybe your spirit is soaring, and you have a great relationship with your partner, but you're struggling with your craft. Maybe you've been under the assumption that all areas of your life were great, but when you did the Life Ladder Assessment, you realized you had forgotten about committing to your community.

If one or more rungs are weak, you'll have a harder time reaching the top of your wall. The Life Ladder Assessment is a tool for determining which rungs of your Life Ladder are healthy and balanced and which ones may need some attention.

MY LIFE LADDER™

Often, when I feel like I am not getting enough done, revisiting My Life Ladder can help me focus on what matters most to me now. Acknowledging my priorities allows me to not stress about areas that aren't as important to me at the moment.

The objective is to look at the rungs of your Life Ladder, then rate each question below based on how you honestly feel—*without judgment*. Read and reflect on each question and write down your score from 1 to 5 (1 = *strongly disagree* and 5 = *strongly agree*).

I recommend completing this tool before you complete your iMpact Planner each quarter. That way, you'll know which rungs need the most of your time and energy. You can then implement action items from your Take 5 Check-In and your 3-3-1 practices to strengthen those rungs.

Examine each rung in the ladder and assess how you feel about your life through this lens. Rate each item from 1 to 5. 1 meaning you are completely off track and 5 meaning you are rocking in this arena in your life.

SPIRIT

The first rung of the ladder. This can have different meanings to each of us. It could be about nature, relationships, or just taking time to stop and breathe. Nurturing the spirit helps me to define what I want from life, what my reason for being is (My Why). Ultimately this is also about realizing there is something greater than me in the universe. My Spirit helps me to know my soul and thus know who I am.

1. I know what spirit is to me and I connect with it daily. _____
2. I am peaceful and am not rushing. _____
3. I know how to focus on the moment and enjoy life. _____
4. I know how to manage my emotions and not let them unduly influence my decisions and actions. _____

TOTAL FOR SPIRIT _____ / 20

HEALTH

The body, as the vessel of the soul, is the means for achieving that which the soul desires. It makes sense that, in order to carry out the soul's desires to the fullest, the vessel must be in optimal working condition. I want to be healthier and live a long life, so keeping my body nurtured with exercise, nutritious foods, and water is imperative.

1. I have a plan and I am working it to optimize my health. _____
2. I get enough sleep and feel energetic in the morning. _____
3. I am confident I will be able to do the things I want past my 80's. _____
4. My energy level is amazing. _____

TOTAL FOR HEALTH _____ / 20

UNSCATTER THE CHATTER

RELATIONSHIPS

What I really look for in my relationships is "my team," a circle of confidantes that I am extremely close to and trust above all others—these are the people that matter most to me. My family, the people that share the same values with me, and those that I enjoy hanging with and working with. As a team, we are able to share a safe space in which we can be open with one another about anything and everything.

> 1. I have 10 trusted relationships that I can share my dreams and fears openly to. _____
>
> 2. I take to heart the open and honest feedback I receive. _____
> 3. I am working with people I love. _____
> 4. I have peer groups that elevate my energy. _____
>
> TOTAL FOR RELATIONSHIPS _____ / 20

CRAFT

There are jobs we all need to make money, and there are careers that we can advance and hopefully love. But having a craft is what is most important. A craft enables you to learn as you teach, to heal as you go—we teach what we need to learn! Craft provides the means to continue growing and advancing. Craft is a means of expressing your passion. Only when you are working within that passion can you say you've found your craft.

> 1. I love all the activities that I am doing, and they give me energy. I know that I am working on my Great Gift. _____
> 2. I have delegated the things I am not good at & don't like. _____
> 3. I am viewed as a thought leader in my profession. _____
> 4. I know, and stay focused on, my goals and objectives (I avoid distractions when necessary). _____
>
> TOTAL FOR CRAFT _____ / 20

MY LIFE LADDER ASSESSMENT™   iMATTER

COMMUNITY

My community can be my neighborhood, my city, and/or my peer groups. It consists of the people I am committed to and want to support. When I am focused and doing good in my community/city/peer group, I feel as though I can make a positive difference. And when I am making a positive difference, I am building and Living My Legacy, Now.

1. I am my authentic self in my communities/world. _____
2. I am a positive contributor to my communities (I work to find solutions to issues). _____

3. I love my neighborhood, my town, or my peer groups. _____
4. I am willing (have the courage) to take a stand for the things I believe in. _____

TOTAL FOR COMMUNITY _____ / 20

You can "score" up to 20 points in each area defined by the rung. You can use these scores to choose where to focus your attention on in the coming days, weeks, or the next quarter. Establish priorities and objectives in each arena accordingly.

Want another way to measure your iMpact?

HOW'D YOU SCORE OVERALL?

0–50: Living an Okay Life
50–80: Living a Good Life
80–100: Living a Great F'ing Life! iM!

It's okay no matter where you are at! Now is the time to begin again and choose where you want to be, or maybe you are already rocking it and loving life!

It's a choice. Are you living a life around "have-tos?" OR are you living into your "love-tos" and what matters most to you and acting like you matter?

APPENDIX C

Dad's Top Ten Lessons for Life

Remember the eulogy I did for my Dad? Here are his top ten lessons of life as I see them.

10. **Be positive**. It will all work out. Move on. That was then; this is now.
9. **Take great vacations**. Really get away and create great memories with your family.
8. **Enjoy nature**. Many of our best vacations were the simplest and involved watching a sunset behind a mountain or lake.
7. **Enjoy sports**. Sports were times to gather as a family to work together as a team, laugh, triumph, or cheer on our team.
6. **Be grateful**. Appreciate one another, your life, and your good fortune.
5. **Keep it simple**. Don't rush. Don't create or participate in drama. Don't worry about what others think. Keep it about a few really important things.
4. **Happy hour**. Make time every day to check in, slow down, and take a deep breath.
3. **Maintain lifelong friendships**. "Lifers," or people who you'd do anything for, and vice versa, are beyond value.
2. **Have a sense of humor**. Laugh at the moment, laugh at life, laugh at ourselves. Don't take things or yourself too seriously.
1. **Family first**—*always*. Dad showed up and was there for our family. He was present, available, and full of unconditional love. He was a servant leader; we were never a burden.

APPENDIX D

The 7 Lifetime Expanders

LIFETIME EXPANDERS™

There are seven key lifetime expanders:

1. CREATE GREAT RELATIONSHIPS
2. CHOOSE YOUR ATTITUDE
3. REALIZE WHAT MATTERS MOST
4. CLARIFY WHO YOU ARE
5. FOLLOW YOUR NORTH STAR
6. LIVE YOUR LEGACY, NOW
7. BE, REGARDLESS

Bibliography

Chapter 4

Walsch, Neale Donald. *Conversations with God: An Uncommon Dialogue, Volume 3*. Newburyport, MA: Hampton Roads, 1998.

Chapter 6

Brown, Brené. "Brené Brown Talks About Vulnerability." International College for Personal & Professional Development (ICPPD). https://icppd.com/brene-brown-talks-about-vulnerability/.

Chapter 7

Ruiz, Don Miguel. *The Four Agreements, A Practical Guide to Personal Freedom*. San Rafael, CA: Amber-Allen Publishing, 1997.

"Another Day," featuring Adam Pascal, Rosario Dawson, Jesse L. Martin, Anthony Rapp & Wilson Jermaine Heredia, MP3 audio, track 10 on *RENT (Original Motion Picture Soundtrack)*, Columbia Pictures, 2005.

Bridge of Spies, directed by Steven Spielberg. Universal Studios, CA: DreamWorks Pictures, 2015.

Singer, Michael Alan. *The Untethered Soul: The Journey Beyond Yourself*. Oakland, CA: New Harbinger Publications, 2007.

Chapter 8

Campbell, Joseph. *The Joseph Campbell Companion: Reflections on the Art of Living*. New York: Harper Collins, 1991.

About the Author

Bob Shenefelt (Coach Bob) is a Visionary leader, keynote speaker, and vibrant entrepreneur. His North Star is elevating the entrepreneurial spirit through self-mastery and connection. He facilitates transformational retreats and coaching experiences. An author of several books, he resides in Birmingham, Michigan, with his wife Sheryl, two phenomenal kids, Grace and Nick, and their beloved dog, Brady.

You can connect with Coach Bob and learn more about the coaching and programs he offers at iMatter.com. Check out his Visionary peer group at TheVisionaryForum.com.

LinkedIn: LinkedIn.com/in/Bob-Shenefelt
Facebook: Facebook.com/iMatterRevolution
Instagram: Instagram.com/iMatterRevolution

GAIN CONFIDENCE, CLARITY & COMMITMENT with our proven iMatter Success System

The Time is NOW to Step into Your Greatness

The Enlightened Visionary 90-Day Boot Camp is all about YOU.

Ready to:
- FEEL fulfilled living your life's purpose?
- DO what you love and are great at?
- TAP into the magic of life?

SPEND TIME with who and what matters most?
Contact admin@imatter.com for more details.
Sign up for *your* Visionary Coaching today at
iMatter.com

Success with Less Stress!

Become a thought leader.
Step into your greatness.
Make a huge difference in the world.

Join other amazing Visionaries for

Community – Growth – Inspiration

90-MINUTE meetings for
EXPONENTIAL BREAKTHROUGHS

- a virtual destination connects you with other kick-ass visionaries you want to know
- experience impactful guest speakers
- *flexible, convenient, no pressure—come when you can*
- exhilarating bi-monthly encounters where Visionaries learn from each other, build relationships, and accept challenges to step into greatness

 Scan this code to apply for a free test drive, or visit:
TheVisionaryForum.com

The VISIONARY Summit
Where Visionaries Connect
TheVisionarySummit.com

Searching for more meaning, magic, and mastery in life?

Join Coach Bob for free training and discover how you can live a great f'ing life!

iMATTER

Here's a sneak peek at what you'll get:

The Simple Daily Practice to Position You for Success
Use Coach Bob's powerful 3-3-1™ practice to set up
your day to be exponentially productive!

The 5-Minute Check-In Exercise to Create Massive Shifts
Get access to one of the most valuable tools Coach Bob
uses to create results for his private clients.

The My Life Ladder™ Method to Create Clarity and Focus
Take the My Life Ladder™ Assessment and
discover what matters most in life.
(It may not be what you think!)

Visit iMatter.com/FreeTraining
to get started today!

Visionary Retreats & Workshops

go to the mountain
connection | clarity | conviction

An exclusive four-day, three-night retreat for

EXPONENTIAL VISIONARIES

or anyone ready to live a great f'ing life and
make a huge difference in the world

Your opportunity to grow in:

Connection with other great visionaries, nature, and yourself!
Clarity around what matters most, who you are, and why you are here.
Conviction to follow your plan, commit to change, and make an impact.

By Application Only
Visit GoToTheMountain.com to
submit yours today!

Also available:
- Creating Great Relationships (business or personal)
- Unscatter the Chatter
- 6 Habits of a Great F'ing Visionary

BLOCKCHAIN
VERIFIED IP

Made in the USA
Middletown, DE
13 October 2022

12600794R00124